JOHN CHARLES FRÉMONT
The Last American Explorer

JOHN CHARLES
Frémont

The Last American Explorer

BY RONALD SYME

Illustrated by Richard Cuffari

William Morrow & Company   New York 1974

Printed in the United States of America.
1   2   3   4   5   78   77   76   75   74

Library of Congress Cataloging in Publication Data

Syme, Ronald (date)
  John Charles Frémont: the last American explorer.

  SUMMARY: A biography of the nineteenth-century soldier, politician, and explorer whose many expeditions helped open up the western territories to settlers.
  Bibliography: p.
  1. Frémont, John Charles, 1813-1890—Juvenile literature.
[1. Frémont, John Charles, 1813-1890. 2. Explorers, American]
I. Cuffari, Richard (date) illus. II. Title.
E415.9.F8S95   1974   979'.02'0924 [B]   [92]
ISBN 0-688-20120-2   74-4198
ISBN 0-688-30120-7 (lib. bdg.)

CONTENTS

JOHN CHARLES FRÉMONT
The Last American Explorer

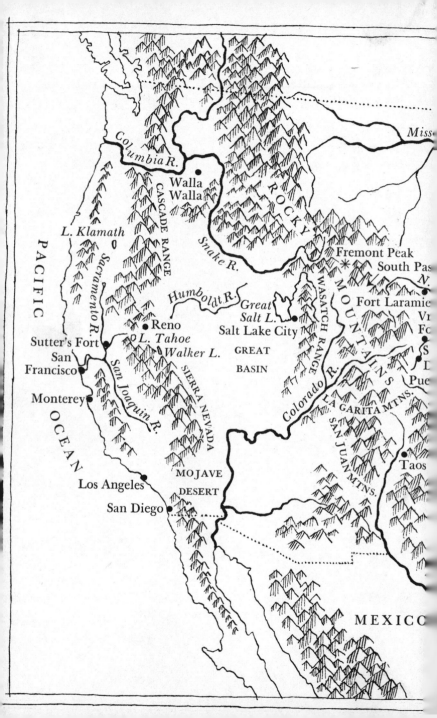

ONE

Frémont

A BOY BESIDE THE SEA

John Charles Frémont was born in Savannah, Georgia, on January 21, 1813. It was a stormy period in American history. The War of 1812 was in progress. Little more than a year later, English officers were to eat President Madison's hastily abandoned dinner in the White House before ordering their troops to set fire to it, the Capitol, and the Library of Congress.

Stormy also were the circumstances surrounding John Charles's birth. His father, Charles Frémon, was a young French aristocrat who had escaped the guillotines of the Revolution by fleeing to America. Among the aristocratic families of Virginia he earned a modest living as a decorative painter and cabinetmaker. Sixteen years later he ran off with Anne Whiting, the bright and attractive daughter of one of the most notable families in the whole of Virginia.

The affair created a tremendous scandal. Anne was married to Major Pryor, a tough, hard-living old Revolutionary War officer. When she left him for Charles Frémon, without obtaining a divorce, the couple had to leave Virginia. In a sturdy carriage drawn by a couple of placid horses they traveled from town to town. Frémon, who was gradually beginning to write his name in the Americanized form of Frémont, found work for his clever hands and artistic gifts wherever they went. The birth of a son did not change their existence. For the first five years of his life, little John Charles Frémont lived like a Gypsy. The family traveled constantly along the dusty white roads that wandered across the still unspoiled American countryside.

Charles Frémon died in 1818. His wife could perhaps have returned to her family. Being proud and independent, however, she was unwilling to do so. Instead, she bought a little boarding house in Charleston, South Carolina, which she proceeded to run with the help of several black servants. There was little money to spare, and Mrs. Frémont could not spend much time with John Charles. But his boyhood in this colorful, gay city of less than 20,000 inhabitants was a pleasant one. French as well as English was still spoken in the streets, and he grew up speaking both languages fluently. By the time he was ten, John Charles was a sunburned, casually dressed little boy, who scampered, shouted, splashed, and fished along the waterfront and reluctantly attended a local school.

The wooden, tarry wharves of Charleston were a captivating place for a youngster, and John Charles was often found near them. One day he helped a prosperous lawyer in the city, John W. Mitchell, locate a ship he sought on a business errand. Mr. Mitchell was impressed with John Charles's quick and courteous ways.

Lawyer Mitchell called on Mrs. Frémont the

next day. "That boy of yours is a most unusual youngster," he said. "I would like to inform you, madam, that if he could acquire a good education there'll be employment for him in my law office. If I may have the privilege of paying his fees, I'd be prepared to send him to a private school."

Thus, when he was fourteen, Charles—as he was called—went off to a preparatory school run by a dry, learned old Scotsman, Dr. Charles Robertson. Dr. Robertson was a tremendous scholar, the author of several textbooks on the classic language of ancient Greece. Digging down into his memory a good many years later, the rather pompous doctor recalled Frémont in the following words:

> He was a youth, apparently about sixteen, or perhaps not as much, of middle size, graceful in manners, rather slender but well-formed, and, upon the whole, what I should call handsome. He had keen, piercing eyes and a high, intelligent forehead.

Any student of those days who wanted to enter college had to pass a preliminary examination in Greek, Latin, and mathematics. Frémont at first seemed rather a hopeless case. He knew only

a few words of Latin and no Greek at all. His knowledge of mathematics was a year or two behind that of all Dr. Robertson's other pupils.

One year after he entered that school Frémont was at the top of his class in Latin. By that time he was also reading books written in classical Greek. In mathematics he was well up to the standard of the rest of the school. Commented Dr. Robertson:

> It seemed to me that young Frémont learned as if by mere intuition. I was myself utterly astonished and at the same time delighted with his progress. . . . I could not help liking him greatly for his gentlemanly conduct and extraordinary progress.

Later he wrote:

> I found it necessary to hire a mathematician to teach both him and myself, for I could not then teach that subject in its higher levels. In this also Frémont made such wonderful progress that at the end of one year he entered the Junior Class in Charleston College while others who had been studying four years or more were obliged to take the Sophomore Class.

Charles Frémon, the father, had never settled

down to anything for very long. Soon it became apparent that his son had inherited the same weakness.

For about a year young Charles did brilliantly in the college classes. Then he began to go to pieces. Probably he was bored. Temperamental, fiery, and independent, Frémont lost interest in his work. He was searching for a change.

He found one, but it was not what he expected. After spending some charming but idle months enjoying the friendship of a French family recently arrived in Charleston, the end came as a shock. He was dismissed from Charleston College only a few months before graduation. Mr. Mitchell, a very disappointed man, lost all interest in him.

Frémont was saved by another fine citizen of Charleston, a Mr. Joel R. Poinsett.

Mr. Poinsett was a brilliantly clever man who had spent some years as American ambassador to Mexico. He was a qualified doctor and also a lawyer. He had crossed the Atlantic in one of the famous Black Ball Line sailing clippers and visited many countries in Europe. While giving a talk to the students at Charleston College, he had been asked a number of intelligent questions by Frémont. A friendship arose between them. But when young Frémont was thrown out of college, Mr. Poinsett was disapproving.

"In South America there is a plant known as the Murderer Vine," he told Frémont. "It grows on trees, saps their life, and eventually brings them crashing down in ruins. Your gay life in Charleston is going to have the same effect on you. You'd be better off away from the city for a while. I will see to it that you're given a chance to leave the place."

At the age of twenty Frémont found himself aboard the American warship, *Natchez*, as a teacher of mathematics. Mr. Poinsett had expertly pulled a few strings.

Off went *Natchez* on a long cruise to South America. Frémont received a steady dose of Navy discipline, which undoubtedly did him no harm at all.

Seven months later a quieter and more thoughtful Frémont returned to Charleston. No one rushed forward to offer him pleasant employment, so he decided to apply for a professorship in the Navy. He passed the examinations and was accepted. But before he had signed the necessary papers, another and more interesting offer came his way. Frémont had reached the turning point in his life.

Captain W.S. Williams, an Army surveyor, had been given the task of surveying the route for a railway planned to run from Charleston to Cincinnati and Louisville. The officer wanted a good, capable assistant with a flair for mathematics. Frémont was just the man for the job. The two of them reached swift agreement.

The Louisville, Cincinnati & Charleston Railroad was willing and eager to pay for the survey work. It had begun operations in Charleston four years earlier, on December 25, 1830. The people of the city were proud of the fact that the first three-and-one-half-ton locomotive, *Best Friend*, had been built in Charleston. The company was prospering and anxious to extend its routes.

Frémont and his companions spent the summer of 1834 working their way across the lovely countryside of the Carolinas and into the cool forested mountains of Tennessee. For the first time in his life Frémont saw the fresh and unspoiled beauty of the interior. Warm and hospitable little farms, wandering white, dusty roads, split-rail fences, and grazing herds of cattle were the only signs of a slowly advancing civilization. At the inns and farmhouses they were given solid meals of fresh meat and vegetables, smoked ham, home-baked bread, fruit, eggs, and creamy milk from the farmyard.

Frémont loved the life. He wrote later, "The survey was a kind of picnic, with enough work to give it zest. We were all sorry when it was over."

Back in the crowded, dusty, colorful streets of Charleston, Frémont no longer felt at home. He was sunburned and fit but ill at ease. The stuffy atmosphere and noise of the city increased his yearning to return to the wilds. Towns and crowded sidewalks were losing their attraction for him. An action recently taken by the American Government was going to enable him to leave.

In 1783, the Cherokee tribe had been granted permanent lands in Georgia. The settlers were still obeying the democratic principles of the founder of their state, the English General James

Oglethorpe. The industrious Indians had created good homes and farms for themselves. They were the best neighbors that any white settler could wish to have. But in 1835, when Frémont was back in Charleston, gold was discovered on Cherokee land. The American Government thereupon ordered the luckless Indians to vacate the territory and move across the Mississippi. In exchange for their losses of farms, homes, growing crops, and prolific fruit trees, the Government made the Cherokees an almost contemptuous payment of five million dollars. Treaties with Indian tribes, apparently, did not have to be honored.

The Government wished to have the region surveyed. Captain Williams was again appointed to undertake the job. Frémont received another invitation to join him.

This time the route lay through wilder, more difficult country. The streams they crossed were wider, deeper, and more swift-flowing. The nights were colder when they reached the forested slopes of the Cumberland Mountains. There were no friendly farmhouses where log fires blazed in great stone hearths. This time the men had to carry their own supplies of flour and sugar and coffee. Meat was no problem. The pine forests were filled with wild hogs. Squatting around the ruddy glow of a campfire while the night wind whimpered through the pine trees, they cooked their pork and coffee and sourdough bread.

The Cherokee Indians they met were sullen, bitter, and unfriendly. Neither Frémont nor his friends could blame them. Frémont himself often attempted to show friendship toward these betrayed Indians, but he thought along the same lines as most other Americans. He could see nothing unjust in the compulsory removal of these Cherokees from their homes and farms.

The survey ended in 1837. Frémont again returned to Charleston. His mother had remarried during his absence, and her name was now Mrs. Sale. His influential friend, Mr. Poinsett, had become Secretary of War under President Van Buren.

Charleston College had awarded Frémont a degree in 1836, and Poinsett had forgiven him for the disappointment of his failure. He invited him to Washington, where he stayed as a guest at the Poinsett home.

The Secretary of War regarded the new Frémont with thoughtful eyes. The handsome young man had grown up considerably. He was quieter, more serious, weatherbeaten, and capable. Captain Williams had spoken most highly of Frémont's services as an assistant surveyor. This, thought Secretary Poinsett, was a young man who could be put to use.

Poinsett knew that the War Department had already planned a survey of the high country between the upper reaches of the Mississippi and Missouri. The man chosen to lead this proposed expedition was an elderly Frenchman, an expert mathematician, who now lived in America. Joseph Nicolas Nicollet had already carried out some excellent survey work along the Arkansas River on behalf of a wealthy fur-trading company. The maps he prepared of this little-known region aroused the admiration of the War Department. Poinsett realized that Nicollet's survey work was far ahead of anything that could be achieved by the Army Topographical Corps. Frémont could consider himself lucky if he were to be trained by such an excellent surveyor. So Poinsett arranged the matter without delay. Frémont became a second lieutenant in the Topographical Corps.

During 1838 and 1839 he worked and studied under the great Nicollet. He became familiar with the wide, yellow-tinged waters of the Mississippi and the high-funneled paddlewheel steamers that thrashed and hooted their way along its surface.

The gracious old city of St. Louis was the starting point for Nicollet's expedition, in which twenty men took part. The survey began as soon as they landed from their steamer at the village of Minneapolis on the Mississippi. The territory that was to become the State of Minnesota in 1858 was then still a thinly settled country, where Sioux encampments abounded and fur traders roamed northward to the Canadian border. Fortified posts were scattered across the plateau of Coteau des Prairies, which lies between the Mississippi and the Missouri. As they approached the arid region that later became South Dakota, the last of the farms was left behind. The Sioux Indians were more plentiful and still living their traditional way of life. Frémont was delighted with them. In November of 1838, he invited a whole encampment of Sioux to go hunting. They crossed into what is now Iowa and killed numbers of elk and deer. In later years Frémont remembered this first hunt. Wistfully he recalled:

> Bright fires, where the venison was roasting, or stewing with corn or wild rice in pots hanging over tripods; squaws busy over the cooking, and children rolling about over the ground. No sleep is better or more restoring than follows such a dinner, earned by such a day.

By the spring of 1838, Nicollet's party was on the Missouri. The voyage was a fine experience for Frémont. The river was flooded with the melting snows of the Rockies, and its channel was harder to follow than usual. With her thirty-foot paddles pounding away at full speed under the mighty thrust of the shining steel cranks, the little riverboat bumped and floundered her way past sandbanks, floating trees, and towheads, sandbars covered with cottonwoods. Toward sunset they would moor to the bank and remain until dawn the following day. Frémont and his companions disembarked at Fort Pierre, in what is now South Dakota. They had completed in seventy-two days a voyage of 1200 miles.

Now they were in buffalo country, and Frémont watched with wondering eyes as vast herds of these ponderous creatures moved leisurely across the level, grassy country that bordered the upper Missouri.

"Were I a young man again," Nicollet said one evening by the campfire, "I would ask nothing better of life than to spend the rest of my days exploring and surveying this vast and majestic country. But this is as far west as I shall ever go. You, Charles, may be the lucky one. Perhaps you will even live to see the western side of yonder Rockies and the blue splendor of the Pacific Ocean. My task is done. But I have taught you most of what I know; perhaps you will carry on from where I leave off."

During the cooler days of autumn, when the night air was turning frosty, the little steamer carried them back to St. Louis. Nicollet's survey was complete. Now he could prepare the first accurate maps of Dakota and Minnesota.

Frémont and Nicollet went together to Washington. They spent their days preparing the official report of their expedition and completing their new maps.

Washington was a dreary little city in those days. There was a single main street, sometimes dusty but ankle deep in mud during rainy weather. There was one small, lamp-lit theater and a few plushy but rather primitive hotels. The social life of the place, such as it was, was restricted to the wealthy families who lived in imposing mansions on the outskirts.

Frémont detested the place. He was accustomed to the gayer, more cosmopolitan, freer life of Charleston. The streets of his native city might be just as dusty or muddy but along them rolled the glistening carriages of the wealthy planters, the wagons bearing bales of cotton or interesting cargoes from seagoing ships. Across the clean ocean came fresh breezes to temper the stagnant heat of the summer months. Washington, he decided, was dull, dreary, overly respectable, and utterly provincial. Twenty-six-year-old Lieutenant Frémont, a dapper, handsome young man with bright blue eyes and curly black hair that was a little too long for an Army officer, was bored. He yearned to go back to the wilderness.

TWO

Benton

A SENATOR'S DAUGHTER

Secretary of War Poinsett had not forgotten his interest in Frémont. He was merely making sure of his reliability before taking his next step to arrange the young man's future. In the meantime, he saw that Frémont had plenty of chances to meet the leading political figures of the day. Among these men was wealthy Thomas Hart Benton, a senator from Missouri.

Critics declared that Benton was an obstinate

fellow, who took himself and his political views much too solemnly. As a result, he had lost any sense of humor he might once have had. Senator Benton's friends, on the other hand, declared that he was a sincere, intelligent, and honorable man.

Both sides were right. Benton was as forthright as a bulldozer. His views on every subject under the sun were about as flexible as a steel girder. Although the inhabitants of Missouri were reputed to have a dry, colorful sense of humor rich with river lore and folk tales, Senator Benton had perhaps lost this quality during the seven years he had spent in the Senate. But no one could dispute the fact that Thomas H. Benton was an entirely honorable man, with a great deal of common sense and that his far-seeing ideas for future national development often turned out to be right.

As far as Frémont was concerned, the most important thing about the Senator was the fact that the youngest of his four daughters was a handsome and intelligent fifteen-year-old girl named Jessie. She was still attending an exclusive private boarding school in neighboring George-town.

Jessie was dark-haired, brown-eyed, and unusually clever. She had inherited her father's obstinacy, but she did have a nice sense of humor —too much so for her father's peace of mind. She had, as an historian noted, "a quality of imagination which the Senator never possessed." To go with her good looks were determination, courage, and a mind of her own.

At first the Senator did not notice that young Frémont's frequent evening visits to the well-disciplined Benton household were not entirely for the pleasure of listening to his political views. With an Army salary scarcely sufficient to keep himself and no definite plans for his future, twenty-eight-year-old Frémont had rashly fallen in love with the charming Jessie.

Senator Benton was not pleased when he realized what had happened. Both he and Mrs. Benton liked Charles Frémont but not to the extent of having him as a son-in-law. After a few heart-to-heart discussions in the book-lined drawing room, Senator Benton announced his verdict: Jessie was to stop seeing Lieutenant Frémont except at social gatherings where they might meet by chance.

Benton then pulled a few strings. Frémont suddenly found himself ordered to make a survey of the Des Moines River in Iowa Territory. And that, thought Senator Benton, would put an end to that. Young Frémont was to be removed from the map. Now it remained merely to deal with Jessie.

Mrs. Benton and Jessie soon were invited to spend a holiday at the Virginia home of Mrs. Benton's family. They would remain there until after a family wedding, planned to take place in a couple of weeks' time. Having thus temporarily placed a distance of 1000 miles between his daughter and Lieutenant Frémont, Senator Benton relaxed.

Frémont spent the next six months on the wide and fertile plains of Iowa Territory. In those days the future state had a total population of 40,000 people. Frémont found neither the work nor the country interesting. He yearned merely to complete his survey as quickly as possible and return to Washington and Jessie Benton.

In the 1840's young ladies were not expected to argue with their parents. Randolph, Senator Benton's only son, was too young to speak up for Charles Frémont, whom he liked. But Jessie, who understood her father very well, began to soften him up when she returned from Lexington, Virginia. She rewrote his speeches in her beautiful, clear handwriting. She brought him books he needed from the shelves of his study and selected daily the flower he wore in his buttonhole. The Senator found that a tray containing cocoa and cakes always arrived regularly on those nights when he was working late in his office. His letters were posted as soon as he had sealed and addressed them.

In September, 1841, Frémont was back in Washington. He and Jessie contrived to meet secretly. They visited a number of clergymen whom they asked to officiate at a secret marriage. But Senator Benton's disapproval of the proposed match was common gossip in Washington by that time. Frémont and Jessie met with one refusal after another.

Finally a Catholic priest, Father Van Horseigh, a friend of Frémont's, agreed to marry them. The marriage took place in a stuffy private room at Gadsby's Hotel on October 19, 1841. Surrounded by curved-legged, plush-covered chairs, heavy velvet drapes, and aspidistras in green glazed bowls, some of Jessie's loyal friends attended to act as witnesses.

As soon as they were married, Jessie returned home. Frémont went to his lodging. The friends sat back and waited to see what would happen.

In November, Jessie and husband Charles decided to break the news. Hand in hand they walked into the Senator's study and told him. History remains silent on the way Senator Benton reacted to the news. He probably said—or shouted—all the things expected of infuriated parents in those stern days. Perhaps he turned purple and pounded his desk. Finally he ended with the customary words: "Leave my house. Never darken my doorway again."

Suddenly remembering the evening tray of cocoa, the flower for his buttonhole, and Jessie's elegant handwriting, the Senator relented slightly. "I refer to this young man who calls himself your husband. You, Jessie, shall remain."

Jessie's own temper suddenly flashed. "If Charles goes," she replied defiantly, "I shall go with him. If he is not to return to this house, neither shall I."

Senator Benton sat down suddenly in his chair. Jessie was his favorite daughter. He was a fair-minded man. Besides, Jessie had made herself indispensable to him. "Very well," he declared, after a brooding silence. "You shall remain here, and your husband may remain with you."

Having unwillingly acquired Charles Frémont as his son-in-law, the Senator wisely decided to make the best of a bad job. Though he went to no personal expense, he found work for Frémont that was destined to be of tremendous value to the United States.

West of the Missouri lay vast territories of prairie and mountain, desert and forest. Fur traders, prospectors, and a few ill-equipped explorers had wandered across those great tracts. The Lewis and Clark expedition had reached the Pacific Ocean in November, 1805. As a result of their achievement, the United States had based certain claims to the territories now known as the States of Washington and Oregon.

About the time that Frémont married Jessie, Senator Benton and his fellow politicians had the idea that England was preparing secret plans to seize both those territories for herself. They were wrong, but Benton and the rest of them believed it. To upset the supposed British plans, the politicians wanted to see a great and endless stream of American settlers pouring westward across the plains and through the Rockies to fill up the empty spaces of Oregon and Washington. In addition, they looked with vaguely defined ambitions toward the Mexican territory of California.

The trouble was, as Benton soon discovered, that there were no reliable maps of the routes that the settlers should follow. The men who knew the trails and the river fords and the landmarks, the grazing grounds, hostile Indian territory, and the deserts, were mostly nearly illiterate, antisocial fellows who preferred to keep their knowledge to themselves. They were content in their log shanties with their guns and their Indian wives. They had no wish to collaborate with Government officials in setting down on paper their knowledge of the locality, or in passing on their hard-won knowledge to others. Not even the great old-time pathfinders, like Jim Bridger or Jedediah Smith—who had crossed the Rockies in 1824—or the great Kit Carson, who could neither read nor write, were interested in

Senator Benton and his ambitious plans. They wanted to be left alone to lead their simple lives. They certainly did not want hordes of greenhorn settlers trailing across the great sweeps of country they had come to regard as their own.

By that year of 1841–1842, Benton realized that no one could expect settlers, accompanied by their wives and children, to take off into wild, unknown country where, while they groped their way, they might be scalped, starved to death, or frozen stiff in a blizzard. These men would demand reliable maps before they started the wheels of their wagons rolling westward. Maps must come first. Then the settlers would follow later.

Benton's sensible views found plenty of support. But President John Tyler, a Virginian socialite, was more interested in the idea of annexing Texas than he was in settlement of the Pacific coast. Besides, he was aware that since 1818 England and the United States had maintained an amicable understanding on the subject of Oregon. The territory reposed under the joint protection of their two countries. After two spells of unpleasantness in the past sixty-five years, relations between the United States and England were at last improving. The President had no wish to see this slowly developing friendship disturbed.

So Benton left the President alone and went to work on his fellow senators. Nicollet, he explained truthfully, was too old to lead a fresh expedition. Young Lieutenant Frémont, who had been trained by the brilliant old Frenchman, would be just the man to replace him. Frémont was a highly skilled surveyor and had already gained much experience during his earlier trips in the wilds.

Accordingly, Frémont was selected to make the first of several planned surveys. He was to proceed westward between the Kansas and Great Platte Rivers to the South Pass through the Rockies. This pass was the one used by Jedediah Smith in 1824 and lay in what is now southwest Wyoming.

The famous old Oregon Trail, which ran northwest from Independence on the Missouri and then up the Platte Valley, used the South Pass on its way to the Columbia Valley. The total length of this journey was about 2000 miles. Its westerly stretch was full of dangers including hostile Indians, undrinkable springs of alkaline water, and the sudden, killing blizzards of the Rockies.

Benton hoped that Frémont might be able to discover a new and safer route. At any rate, he would be able to prepare better maps of the areas he traversed than any existing at that time.

Seven months after his marriage to Jessie Benton, in May, 1842, Frémont set off for St. Louis where he would assemble the men of his expedition. He traveled the first part of the way by railroad. The coaches, in which passengers sometimes nearly froze to death or sweated in the tremendous heat, were rattling little wooden boxes, almost springless, attached to rumbling iron wheels. From Cincinnati he voyaged down the Ohio and then up the Mississippi to St. Louis.

The flimsy, brightly painted riverboat, which resembled a pink-and-white birthday cake afloat, was some improvement on the railroad but not much. The private cabins were poorly built, and the woodwork groaned and squeaked with every revolution of the pounding engine. On the lower deck were crowded emigrants, frontiersmen, trappers, sun-bleached prospectors, and farmers

wearing stiff new store clothes. In the middle of that deck, unprotected except for a light wooden rail, was the main engine. The passengers slept, ate, and played cards beside the great whirling cranks that drove the paddlewheels. It was all very primitive, new, and exciting.

Frémont began to assemble his party in St. Louis. Nineteen Canadian *voyageurs*, all of them veterans of river and forest, were the first to be selected. They were easygoing but temperamental fellows, who could endure endless hardship but fly into a violent rage over a small grievance. Being half-French himself, Frémont knew how to get along well with them. Next came a fair-haired, blue-eyed German topographer named Charles Preuss. He was a skilled artist, a reasonable surveyor, and had a most unexpected sense of humor. In later years Preuss was to become one of Frémont's most trusted companions, although there were occasions when the sturdy little German privately disapproved of Frémont's actions.

Lucien Maxwell was the son of a wealthy merchant. A desk and a high stool in a stuffy office were not for him. He had taken to the frontier life and was now engaged as a hunter for the party. By good luck Frémont then met Kit Carson, whom he promptly hired as a guide. This famous frontier scout was then thirty-two years old. He was only of middle height but enormously wide in the shoulders and deep in the chest. Frémont found it hard to believe that this quiet-spoken, polite, and peaceful man was known as one of the toughest and most experienced Indian fighters alive.

But no skirmishes with war parties were to be expected during the coming trip. Most of the way would lie through regions that already contained a scattered population on lonely farms and in military outposts. Frémont allowed his young brother-in-law, Randolph Benton, to accompany the expedition. The boy was only twelve years old but quick to realize that he was being given a chance to see a vanishing way of life.

Eight mule carts were to go with the expedition. The rest of the men were mounted on horses. Most of them carried French Minié rifles. The muzzle-loading rifle was a tremendous improvement over the older smoothbore muskets, but it was still a ponderous weapon by modern standards. It weighed 10½ pounds, had a barrel 39 inches long, and a bore of .702 inches. The recoil from a Minié rifle would have knocked young Benton flat on his back if he had ever tried to fire one.

Frémont led the expedition out of St. Louis at the beginning of June, 1842. He was heading for the Kansas River. The men had not settled down yet to camp routine and each other's ways. Preuss, with a German passion for neatness, disapproved of conditions and said so in his private diary.

> During the night a lot of rain, which made me get up. Everything wet . . . what a disorder in this outfit; dirty cooking. To be sure, how can a foolish lieutenant manage such a thing.

Clearly Frémont still had a lot to learn. He was inclined to be careless about details, to trust too much to luck, and had not yet developed the habit of maintaining discipline and tidiness among his men.

Kit Carson had lived for years in the wilds. He was just the opposite of Frémont. Whatever he was doing, whether stalking a buffalo or bedding down for the night, he thought ahead. In his mind there was always an alternative plan ready for use in an emergency. Thus, even in the safe country through which they were passing, Kit Carson so placed his saddle when he lay down that it protected his head against a sudden blow. His pistol lay tucked under the saddle. His rifle, at half cock, lay warm and dry beside him under his blanket. When sitting beside the campfire, Carson never gazed into the flames. His eyes were thus able to adjust quickly to the darkness of the night. By his own example, Carson, without reproving and lecturing his leader, gradually taught Frémont a great deal more about looking after himself and his men.

Once the expedition reached the eastern prairie of Kansas, Carson insisted on the carts being drawn in a circle around the nightly camp. The tents were pitched inside this barricade. The horses and mules were hobbled and grazed while a sentry guarded them. As daylight faded, the men cooked and ate their supper. The animals were tethered to the wagons, the fires were extinguished, and the sentries posted.

Inflatable rubber boats were a newfangled idea, and Frémont had included one of these handy little craft with his stores. They tested it for the first time when crossing the Kansas River at a point where the stream was 100 yards wide. The precious surveying instruments were placed in the boat and the river safely crossed. Then Frémont, in one of his fits of impatience, overloaded the boat for the second trip. This time the boat capsized and supplies were lost or so spoiled as to be unusable.

For the next three months Frémont continued to carry out his mission, to prepare a report on the "rivers and country between the frontiers of Missouri and the base of the Rocky Mountains; and to examine the character and ascertain the latitude and longitude of South Pass, the great crossing-place in these mountains on the way to Oregon."

The men grew sunburned and ragged as they moved westward. They were eating so much rich meat that many of them began to suffer from boils and upset stomachs. Carson promptly brewed a concoction of chokecherries and certain herbs. It tasted terribly bitter and the men detested it, but the brew proved an excellent cure.

At length they came to the fast-running Platte River. They began to follow its course westward to the Rocky Mountains, across a countryside that bore signs of having once been thickly populated with Indians. Grapes, plums, and gooseberries grew wild in this region, and the men rejoiced as they stewed the fruit in their cooking pots.

Frémont was so busy with his surveying instruments that he was seldom as careful as he should have been of his own safety. Sometimes he allowed the rest of his men to ride on while he remained behind. It was a foolish practice anywhere in Indian country, and on one occasion it nearly caused his death. One day he was alone with Maxwell, the hunter, when they suddenly saw a band of Indians riding toward them. Frémont described the encounter:

> At first they did not appear to be more than fifteen or twenty, but group after group darted into view at the top of the hills. They numbered two or three hundred, naked to the breechcloth. The

timber we were endeavoring to make was on the opposite side of the river. Before we could make the bank, down came the Indians upon us.

I am inclined to think that in a few seconds more, the leading man, and perhaps some of his companions, would have rolled in the grass; for we had jerked the covers from our guns and our fingers were on the triggers. . . . Just as he was about to fire, Maxwell recognized the leading Indian and shouted at him in the Indian language: "You're a fool; don't you know me?"

The sound of his own language surprised the Indian. He swerved his horse a little and passed us like an arrow. He wheeled as I rode out to him and gave me his hand, striking his breast and exclaiming "Arapahó!" They proved to be a village of that nation among whom Maxwell had resided a year or two earlier as a trader.

Preuss was enjoying himself, but he spent much time wondering whether the latest Indian visitors were awaiting their chance to scalp him. His diary entry for the ninth of July notes:

Daily, several people, white and Indian, have been killed in the country now lying to the west of us. If our party cannot be increased at Fort Laramie (on the North Platte River) it would be best to turn back and limit ourselves to the survey of the Platte.

... It would be ridiculous to risk the lives of twenty-five people just to determine a few longitudes and latitudes and to find out the height of a mountain range. The men are not at all inclined to continue without reinforcements. In a few days everything will be settled at Laramie. I hope we shall get that far safely.

Within the heavy, timbered walls of Fort Laramie, which they reached on July 15, 1842, Frémont received confirmation of the Indian danger. Several Indian chiefs came to see him. They were grave, dignfied, elderly men whose names included the Otter Hat, Breaker of Arrows, Black Night, and Bull's Tail.

"You have come among us at a bad time," they said. "Some of our people have been killed, and our young men have gone into the mountains to avenge the blood of their relations which has been shed by the whites. Our young men are bad. If they meet you they will believe that you are carrying goods and ammunition to their enemies, and they will fire on you."

If Frémont had turned back on receiving this warning, the decision might have affected the rest of his career. But the reply he made to the chiefs was recorded in his report. It aroused the admiration of Senator Benton and his friends and increased their respect for him.

"When you told us that your young men would kill us," said Frémont, "you did not know that our hearts are strong. You did not see perhaps the rifles which my young men carry in their hands. We are few and you are many. You may kill us all, but there will be much crying in your villages, for many of your young men will not return from the mountains. When the sun is ten paces higher, we shall be on the march. We may throw away our lives, but we will not turn back."

THREE

Carson

THE DANGEROUS RIVER

Frémont went on up the North Platte River. His men were by no means happy. It was all right, they declared, for Frémont to show such courage, but what they wanted was a peaceful existence. They were jumpy, nervous, and irritable. Whenever one of them paused to remove prickly pear thorns from his feet, he insisted that all his companions remain with him until the operation was finished. Holding their rifles ready, the men nerv-

51

ously eyed nearby clumps of ash, red elm, and cottonwood as if expecting an Indian war party to appear from cover at any moment.

The outward stage of Frémont's mission had now been reached. Ahead of them lay the cloud-veiled, majestic barrier of the Rockies. They climbed the broad, pebbly track that led into the wide, easy entrance to the South Pass. Snow-covered mountains rose on each side of this passage, but the track itself reached a maximum height of only 7000 feet. The ascent was so gradual that Frémont, who was busy with his surveying instruments, found it hard to decide the actual spot where gushing, icy streams began to flow westward toward the distant Pacific instead of toward the east.

The weather was clear and bright but terribly cold. Even in the daytime the thermometer rose only a degree or two above freezing. While they were still in the South Pass, frequent hailstorms lashed their leather-and-wool protected bodies. They were forced to take shelter behind rocks to protect themselves, for the hailstones were often as large as musketballs, or more than half an inch in diameter.

Frémont had not been as careful as he should have been to make sure that the men's rations were adequate. Days had now passed since they had eaten the last fragment of bread. Ham and bacon were finished. Coffee and sugar were running short and were severely rationed. The men's daily meals consisted almost entirely of dried buffalo meat cooked in buffalo fat. The only fresh meat they obtained was when Carson or Maxwell—the two best shots—managed with their Minié rifles to bring down one of the big-horned sheep that bounded gracefully from rock to rock or paused to peer at the distant men from behind a sparse screen of pine trees. But the flesh of these animals was tough and had a peculiar flavor. A number of the men, including young Randolph Benton, were unable to eat it.

When they had noted the latitude and longitude of South Pass, Frémont turned to explore the range to the north. In the foreground towered the massive spire of a single peak, which fascinated Frémont from the moment he first saw it silhouetted against a shining blue-and-white background.

Accompanied by four men he set out to climb

it. With him went Preuss and three *voyageurs*, Lambert, Janisse, and Basil Lajeunesse, one of the best men in the expedition. Describing his experience later, Frémont wrote:

> I sprang upon the summit and another step would have caused me to fall into an immense snowfield five hundred feet below. To the edge of this field was a sheer icy precipice. I was standing on a narrow crest about three feet in width. . . . As soon as I had gratified the first feelings of curiosity, I descended, and each man ascended in his turn; for I would only allow one at a time to mount the unstable and precarious slab, which it seemed a breath would hurl into the depths below. . . . We met no sign of animal life, except a small bird having the appearance of a sparrow, but while we were resting, a solitary bumble-bee came winging his flight from the eastern valley and lit on the knee of one of the men.

Preuss, who had been an enthusiastic mountaineer in his native Germany, was less frightened of heights than of painted Indians with tomahawks. But he was still having to change his ideas, even at this stage of the trip. On August 12, he had written in his diary:

> As interesting as the mountains are, they cannot

at all be compared to the Alps in Switzerland. No glaciers, ice lakes, avalanches, or waterfalls are to be seen. A little snow on the peak—that is all.

This was before Preuss had scaled the 13,730-foot mountain that was to become known in later years as Fremont's Peak. On August 17, he wrote:

> With the first steps I could dig my heels into the snow; then it became harder. I slipped, sat down on my pants, and slid downhill at a great speed. Although I made all efforts to hold back by trying to dig my fingers into the icy crust, I slid down about two hundred feet, until the bare rocks stopped me again.

Thankfully the men descended to lower altitudes where deer were more plentiful and they could eke out their diet with wild currants, onions, and the artichokes that the pocket gophers hoard in their underground nests.

The Platte River was a wild and angry stream at the best of times. When they arrived on August 23, 1842, it was in flood. The current was tearing along, ripping at the riverbanks and lashing angrily against projecting rocks. A more cautious explorer would have continued overland.

Frémont, in a mood of unwise haste, decided to go down it by boat. On hearing this decision, the *voyageurs*—experienced rivermen in their native Canada—glanced at each other and shrugged their shoulders.

Frémont ordered most of the party to carry on by land and to meet him at Goat Island some twenty miles farther downstream. He himself, accompanied by Preuss and three of the *voyageurs*, embarked in the frail rubber boat. Recklessly, Frémont arranged that a number of surveying instruments, most of his journals, four guns, and a telescope should go in the rubber boat. "We paddled down the river rapidly," said Frémont, "for our little craft was light as a duck on the water. The sun had risen some time earlier when we heard before us a hollow roar."

"*Nous allons arriver à une chute d'eau*," exclaimed Lajeunesse quickly. "We're coming to a rapid."

He made a couple of swift strokes with his paddle to turn the boat toward the shore. Lajeunesse knew all about birchbark canoes and rapids; he did not fancy trying to shoot a rapid in a bouncy, erratic rubber dinghy.

But Frémont lacked experience. He had the overconfidence of youth and ignorance. "We'll trust to the boat," he said. "Keep her in mid-stream."

The rushing torrent swept into a high-walled canyon. Rocky walls rose perpendicularly on either side. Their upper edges curved out of the water, so that the effect was almost to create a tunnel. The men saw that a short distance ahead the river took a sharp turn to the left. They realized that they were in trouble. The descending current was piling against the right-hand wall in a boiling surge and rolling backward off the rocky face in a series of short, sharp, angry waves.

"*On va se baigner*," Lajeunesse said calmly. "We're going to take a bath." He picked up the fifty-foot length of coiled rope that he had quietly prepared for just this emergency.

The boat whirled past a tiny rocky beach lying at the foot of the wall of rock. Lajeunesse made a tremendous leap. The other two *voyageurs* jumped with him. They splashed into shallow water, scrambled ashore, and began to hang onto the rope, the other end of which was made fast to the bow of the boat.

The immense pull of the current proved too great for them to check the boat's sweeping rush. The two other *voyageurs* were forced to let go of the rope. Lajeunesse held on a moment too long. He was dragged into the rushing, icy water and carried downstream after the vanishing boat. On seeing their companion thus departing, the remaining two *voyageurs* jumped in after him.

Frémont suddenly noticed another tiny beach some distance ahead. He called to Preuss to seize a paddle and help him to steer the boat toward it. A fortunate eddy also helped. The boat banged onto the rocky shelf, whereupon Frémont leaped ashore and hung onto the bow with all his strength. Preuss joined him at once. They dragged the boat almost clear of the water. Then Lajeunesse arrived, followed by his two half-drowned companions. One of these men, Descoteaux, was unable to swim yet in some extraordinary way he had managed to remain more or less afloat while being swept downstream. He was, however, well waterlogged by the time Lajeunesse grabbed him by his shoulder-length hair.

"Best hang on tightly," gasped Descoteaux,

"otherwise, Basil, you'll never get that five dollars I owe you!"

After this escape, most men would have preferred to seek some path leading from the beach to the top of the gorge. Frémont believed that to continue their journey overland would be a slow way to rejoin their comrades at Goat Island. With almost incredible rashness he ordered the men to re-embark, and they pushed off once more. As the *voyageurs* grimly expected, they were soon in trouble again. Frémont reported their next adventure:

> The boat struck a concealed rock at the foot of the fall which whirled her over in an instant. My first feeling was to assist the men and save some of our effects; but a sharp concussion or two convinced me that I had not yet saved myself. A few strokes brought me into an eddy, and I landed on a pile of rocks on the left side. Looking round I saw that Preuss had gained the same shore on the same side about twenty yards below. . . . On the opposite side, against the wall, lay the boat, bottom up; and Lambert was in the act of again saving Descoteaux, whom he had grasped by the hair, and who could not swim. . . . For a hundred yards below, the current was covered with floating books and boxes,

bales of blankets, and scattered articles of clothing; and so strong and boiling was the stream that even our heavy instruments, which were all in cases, kept on the surface.

Frémont had learned a fresh lesson. It was one that he never forgot. The beach on which they landed had a narrow path leading to the top of the canyon. The soaked, bruised, and shivering men made their way up it. They started a fire and began to dry their clothes. It was thanks to the *voyageurs* that much of the equipment was saved from the Platte River. Lajeunesse came ashore with Frémont's double-barreled gun. On a second trip he rescued some of the blankets. But most of the surveying instruments, including the telescope, were gone for good. So were some of Frémont's journals, a box containing three compasses, and all the emergency stocks of food they had brought with them.

The boat was badly torn and useless. Not even Frémont wanted to have anything more to do with it. Limping, tired, and hungry, the men walked the rest of the way to Goat Island, where they found the main party awaiting them. It was no easy journey for Frémont, who had lost one of his moccasins in the water and had to pause frequently to remove the thorns of prickly pear.

Preuss had managed to hang on to his precious leather-bound journal while scrambling in and out of the Platte River. He wrote down his experiences at a later date, and he was not in a forgiving mood when he did so, observing:

> It should be noted that we could not have gotten through with the boat, regardless of the disaster. For a distance of four to five miles the river flows through rocks and has falls and rapids of various heights. I don't know how we could have gotten boats and luggage across those rocks. It was certainly stupid of the young chief to be so foolhardy where the terrain was so completely unknown.

After the men had rested and sorted themselves out, they continued their eastward journey. On the site of the future city of Denver, among the snowcapped peaks of the Rockies, they shot a buffalo and made camp for a night. Then they continued on their way through the grassy sandhills of what is now western Nebraska and emerged onto the central plains. Firewood was almost unobtainable, and food had to be cooked with buffalo chips. Not that there was much left to cook. They had now run out of sugar, coffee, and tobacco. Young Randolph Benton was lean and sunburned but in excellent health; the shortage of food scarcely seemed to worry him. But the older men were tired and irritable. Two of the *voyageurs* had a fist fight after some trivial squabble, and Frémont had to separate them. Rattlesnakes abounded, and small, loitering groups of Pawnee Indians made constant efforts to pilfer anything that was not closely guarded.

The dreary marches ended on September 30, 1842. Toward sunset that evening they sighted groves of oak trees along the banks of the Missouri. At dawn the following morning the sound of distant cowbells came clearly through the still, chilly air. The cattle belonged to the first settlers, who had built their homes and run their fences close to the reassuring stockade of the American Fur Company's trading post at Bellevue.

On that particular morning, the farmers were surprised to receive visits from bearded, tattered men who, with money in their hands, hungrily demanded chickens, eggs, cheese, coffee, ham, vegetables, everything that their ill-nourished stomachs yearned for.

Then the expedition went down the Missouri to St. Louis. The men were paid off, and Frémont, accompanied by Randolph Benton, traveled on to Washington.

He reported his return to Colonel J.J. Abert, his superior officer, and hastened to the Benton home to surprise his wife, who had had no word of him. A few days later, on November 13, 1842, Elizabeth Benton Frémont was born.

Senator Benton was in a happy mood. The way the expedition had turned out delighted him. Frémont had taken thousands of observations from which accurate maps of certain parts of the Western regions could be prepared. His careful notes in the journals rescued from the North Platte River described the appearance and gave much valuable information of the country through which they had passed. When these reports and maps were published, they would provide encouragement for westward migration, exactly as the Senator had wanted.

"Much better than anything that's been available in the past," Benton said approvingly to Frémont. "Some of the earlier explorers and geographers took reasonably accurate notes of latitude and longitude but omitted to describe the regions through which they passed. Others wrote long descriptions of rivers and mountains and prairies but omitted their latitudes and longitudes. Settlers going west would have had to carry a whole library of reference books in their wagons in order to find out everything they wanted. The Government will produce your report in one single volume. It'll be just what we've wanted for so long."

All that winter Frémont worked on the preparation of the report. Jessie helped him with much of the actual writing. She had a graceful literary style and an excellent vocabulary. Her imagination helped with the descriptions of scenes and incidents, which her husband sometimes found hard to put into words. The manuscript was finished by the spring of 1843. By that time Benton and his friends had devised a fresh expedition for Frémont.

The new plan was for Frémont to go westward into Oregon. The Oregon Trail would then be surveyed and mapped along its entire length, from the settlement of Independence on the Missouri to the Platte River and along its course into the

Rockies, where settlers used South Pass, and on via the Snake River to the Columbia Valley in Oregon. This 2000-mile trail was still very inadequately mapped.

It was privately suggested to Frémont that once he reached Oregon he might take a quick look at the Mexican territory of California. If possible, he was to report on conditions in the almost unknown Great Basin, which lay between the western flank of the Rockies and the Sierra Nevada.

"The sooner you can complete your mission, the happier we will be," declared Benton. "Migration toward the West is increasing all the time. People are making for the Columbia Valley as best they can at the rate of about a thousand every year. We don't know what happens to most of them; we only hear from time to time of some of those who run into trouble on the way, get themselves lost, or die. Another report like your first one will be of tremendous value to everyone."

Once again Frémont said good-bye to Jessie and her family. He traveled westward by rattling train and churning river steamer until he reached Kansas City in May, 1843. In those days the place consisted of a few scattered houses, two saloons, a muddy street along which hens and ducks wandered freely, and a wooden wharf projecting into the debris-filled waters of the Missouri.

Preuss hurried back to rejoin the new expedition. In spite of his grumbles and fears during the first trip he had enjoyed the freedom and open-air life of the interior. It had become impossible for him to settle down in civilization.

Basil Lajeunesse also rejoined with five of his old companions. Another volunteer was eighteen-year-old Jacob Dodson, a free Negro, a cheerful, powerful, capable man with a sense of humor. Thomas (Broken Hand) Fitzpatrick was to serve as hunter and guide. Frémont hoped that somewhere around the Platte he would meet up with his friend, Kit Carson. The scout had no use for trains and towns and streets. He preferred to remain where the wind blew freshly and nature had not been twisted and sullied by civilization.

Forty men besides their leader composed the second expedition. Stores and tents were carried on twelve carts, each drawn by two mules. A light, well-sprung cart was also used for the scientific instruments and books.

A strange item taken along at Frémont's wish was a ponderous little brass howitzer, a short-barreled cannon used for firing at sharp elevation over short distances. The gun, which fired a twelve-pound shot, had been "borrowed" from the War Department. It was mounted on a handy wheeled carriage, but the seasoned frontiersmen eyed the contraption with disgust. Most of them were carrying the new Hall's breech-loading single-shot carbines of .57 caliber. They were confident that with these weapons they could handle any Indian war party. The howitzer, they thought rightly, was going to be a sight more trouble than it was worth. Frémont would have done better to have left it in the War Department's armories.

On May 20, a hastily written note arrived from Jessie. It was brought overland by a *voyageur* joining the expedition at the last moment. "Depart without delay," wrote eighteen-year-old Jessie. "Everything will be in ruins if you remain any longer where you can be reached by official correspondence."

Jessie's quick eyes and ears had picked up alarming news in Washington. Colonel Abert,

Frémont's superior officer, had found out about the howitzer and wanted Frémont to return to Washington at once in order to give an explanation. Another officer would be sent to take command of the expedition. The letter from Colonel Abert was somewhere in the mail between Washington and Kansas City.

Frémont took his expedition out of Kansas City at a speed that surprised them. He did not relax until they were following the upper reaches of the Kansas River across a dismal, arid plain, where the lightest breeze stirred rolling clouds of dust. Once the river was left behind, the men began to suffer from thirst. The only water they found for several days was in the occasional ponds where rain had collected. Herds of buffalo chose to wallow in these ponds almost daily.

On July 4, 1843, they reached Vrain's Fort. It stood less than fifty miles to the north of the present-day city of Denver. The place in those days was merely a privately owned fur-trading post. The surrounding countryside was filled with deer, bear, mountain lion, elk, and wolves.

Out of this wilderness appeared Kit Carson, pack on saddle and rifle in holster. He and Frémont met within the hospitable walls of the fort, where the men were resting for a few days and enjoying an unlimited supply of fresh, pure water.

"You'd best head for South Pass again," suggested Carson. "It's the only way to get through the Rockies that I know."

Frémont, who was gradually learning to listen to those more experienced than himself, took Carson's advice. He proceeded on a northwesterly course after leaving the fort. It was unfortunate that he had failed to find a new and better route to Oregon along this first section of the trail. The arid area through which they had passed would remain an ordeal for heavily laden wagons accompanied by raw and inexperienced settlers.

They went through South Pass without any trouble. On August 21, they reached the fertile and picturesque valley of Bear River, the principal tributary of Great Salt Lake, where they came upon a large encampment of emigrants, whose white-covered wagons dotted the edge of the wood for several miles along the river. They had been camping there for several days, resting and feeding up their animals before the next stage of their journey, hard travel along the banks of the upper Columbia. These emigrants were the lucky, or more skilled, ones who had made the journey successfully along the Oregon Trail.

On September 6, Frémont reached Great Salt Lake. Being short of provisions at the time—Frémont's expeditions were always running short of food—the men celebrated the fact by eating an evening meal of stewed skunk. By way of an additional delicacy they had some *kooyah*, Indian tobacco root, which poor Preuss, who respected his own healthy stomach, labeled "an indescribably disgusting food."

Frémont was not distracted by the food, however, from investigating Great Salt Lake:

> Hitherto this lake had been seen only by trappers, wandering through the country in search of new beaver streams, caring very little for geography. Its islands had never been visited. . . . Among the trappers, including those in my own camp, were many who believed that somewhere on its surface was a terrible whirlpool, through which the waters found their way to the ocean through some underground cave.

Naturally Frémont wanted to see the whirlpool for himself. He inflated their new rubber boat with the intention of launching it on the lake without delay. But the boat, like so much else about his expedition, had been obtained without carefully checking its quality. The thing was rubbish. Frémont and Carson found out this fact for themselves.

> Two of the air cylinders leaked so much that one man had to remain at the bellows all the time in order to keep them full of air to support the boat. Although we had made a very early start, we loitered so much on the way—stopping every now and then, and floating silently along, to get a shot at a goose or a duck—that it was late in the day when we reached the outlet. . . . We encamped on a low point among rushes and young willows, where there was a quantity of driftwood, which served for our fire. The evening was mild and clear; we made a pleasant bed of the young willows; enough geese and ducks had been killed for an abundant supper at night and for breakfast next morning. The stillness of the water was enlivened by millions of waterfowl.

On September 12, 1843, Frémont was again on his way westward. The food situation was rapidly growing worse, and it was seldom that the men came across any game to shoot. The day after leaving Great Salt Lake, Preuss wrote sadly in his diary, "Last night we devoured seagulls, the only thing we could shoot." Things got even worse during the next few days. A horse had to be shot, and Preuss, who was inclined to be fussy, was revolted by the sight of the dark, lean meat, almost free from fat. He lived on chocolate and coffee for the next twenty-four hours. A passing Indian then sold them some fresh antelope meat, and Preuss was able to sit down to a plate of food of which he approved.

They carried on into the mountainous expanse of the future state of Idaho. With the howitzer still trundling along behind them, they finally reached Fort Hall on the Snake River. This post belonged to the Hudson's Bay Company and was manned by Englishmen.

"You're traveling late in the year," they warned Frémont. "There'll be deep snow soon in the mountains ahead of you. It would be safer to remain here and cross the ranges next spring."

It was good advice, but Frémont was not in a mood to listen. The weather was growing colder daily, and the lowering skies were dark and snow-filled. Some of his men eyed the threatening signs and became dubious. A number of them declared bluntly that they had endured enough. Eleven of them, including Basil Lajeunesse, who wanted to be with his family on their little farm in Missouri, decided to return eastward. Frémont and the rest of his expedition carried on into the mountains.

Twelve miles after they had left Fort Hall they were caught in a snowstorm and forced to make camp for themselves. By way of a change, however, they had enough to eat. The Englishmen had supplied them with dried soup, sugar, coffee, tobacco, flour, and a couple of barrels of salted beef. Even so, conditions in that hasty camp were bad. Frémont never learned to look after his men's shelter and food well. It remained his great weakness as an explorer.

They passed through the westward Sierras with less trouble than they had feared. The mountains were covered with snow, the trail was rocky and ice-covered in places, and the nightly camp was invariably an untidy shambles. A freezing, pitiless wind whistled down from the high crests, and the ill-protected animals suffered so greatly at night that they lost condition. A more prudent explorer would have seen that horses and mules were given at least some shelter on these bitter nights, but Frémont neglected this precaution.

The bad times ended on October 25, 1843. They emerged from the last pass at Walla Walla into the warmer region of what is now the State of Washington. There they caught their first sight of the swift-flowing Columbia River. The wind dropped, the sun shone more warmly, and the animals grazed happily in the luxuriant grass. That night, as they ate salmon, beef, and some of the butter they had been given at Fort Hall, the men quickly forgot the hardships of the past few days. Frémont had not yet experienced the great danger of passing through the mountains in winter.

FOUR

Sutter

MOUNTAIN BLIZZARD

Warmed by the wintry sun, rested, and well fed, Frémont prepared to begin his return journey toward the end of November, 1843. He had no intention of going back along the route by which they had come. His curiosity made him eager to carry out Senator Benton's plan that he should try to find out something about the Great Basin of Nevada. It was an area of which even the

76

toughest prospectors fought shy. Hardened old Jedediah Smith had come south from Great Salt Lake with a small party in 1826. He had successfully trudged westward across the Mojave Desert and emerged from it on the site of Los Angeles. But no one had ever tried to cross the Great Basin from north to south. Frémont decided to attempt the feat. His decision nearly started a mutiny among his men.

They were hardly to blame. Plenty of stories —none of them pleasant—were told about the Great Basin. There were said to be rivers that disappeared, campfires that gleamed brightly in the darkness but disappeared when the exhausted traveler approached them, and daytime heat that caused a man's skin to crack and his senses to reel. These unpleasant wastes, it was generally known, were haunted by nomadic Indians of the most murderous tendencies. Frémont's men from Canada and the fertile Eastern states wanted nothing to do with such horrors.

Even Frémont took unusual precautions. He procured 100 fresh horses and mules from the local Indians. He also obtained a number of Indian guides, some of whom he hoped would be reliable. He bought fresh food supplies from Fort Vancouver on the coast, so there was a reasonable prospect of his men being able to eat better than usual during their crossing of the Great Basin.

They set off southward along the eastern flank of the Cascade Mountains. It was now December, and the weather was growing colder all the time. When they reached the site of Reno, in western Nevada, Frémont had a fresh idea. He would abandon, at least for the time being, his idea of crossing the Great Basin from north to south. Instead, he would turn westward across the Sierras and take a quick look at the Mexican state of California. He knew that the Government of Mexico had recently passed a law that prohibited Americans from entering the state. Like many other Americans, Frémont decided to ignore this restriction.

Somewhere a little south of Lake Tahoe in western Nevada, Frémont found an Indian who spoke lightly of the ease with which he could guide the white men through the westerly mountains.

"But not at this time of the year," said the Indian sternly. "I would not go with you while the snow lies so deep and the wind brings pain to a man's body. Only a madman would try to cross the mountains now. A wise man remains in his tent and smokes his pipe beside a warm fire."

As impatient and ardent as ever, Frémont took it upon himself to ignore this sound advice. He rallied his grumbling men, loaded the patient animals, and took off blithely toward the pass that the Indian had described to him. (Only three years later, a large party of settlers froze to death in this same pass.)

On January 5, 1844, Preuss confided to his diary:

> We've been sitting for three days, wrapped in fog, on a miserable plateau surrounded by bare hills. The animals are dying one after the other. Very little grass, snow instead of water.

The journey went on under similar conditions during the next two weeks. The weather was dreadful. The horses and mules continued to starve or to freeze to death, and the men grew increasingly exhausted. Their longing to turn back—which a wiser man like Carson would have done—made them unwilling to start each day's journey still deeper into those awful mountains. Frémont's entry for January 29 reads:

> Foreseeing the inevitable delay which the how-itzer would subject us to, I reluctantly decided to leave it where it was for the time. . . . We left it to the great sorrow of the party, who were grieved to part with a companion which had made the whole distance from St. Louis.

One very much doubts if the men were nearly so upset as Frémont imagined at leaving this brute of a gun behind. The thing had been nothing but trouble, and it had caused much delay ever since they had left the plains behind.

Preuss noted on February 3:

> The snow is terribly deep, and we can make only a few miles every day. I am almost barefoot. [His boots had worn out.] This surpasses every discomfort that I have experienced so far. . . . Here a buffalo hide is spread on the snow—that is my feather bed.

A week later the party was completely snowed up. By some carelessness no salt had been included with the provisions, and the men were suffering badly from the lack of it. The deficiency was merely another of the misfortunes that were now so numerous that even Frémont might have decided to turn back. As Frémont later recounted in his memoirs:

> Our Indian guide [not the sensible one who preferred to smoke his pipe beside a fire], who understood even more readily than ourselves, and believed the situation hopeless, covered his head with a blanket and began to weep and lament. "I wanted to see the whites," he said, "and I came away from my people to see the whites, but I wouldn't care to die among them. But here . . . !" and he looked around into the cold night and gloomy forest and drawing his blanket over his head, began again to lament.

There was a sequal to this incident two days later.

> Our guide was standing by the fire with all his finery on. Seeing him shiver in the cold, I threw on his shoulders one of my blankets. We missed him a few minutes after and never saw him again. He had deserted.

Frémont and Carson decided to go forward

alone the next day to examine the route ahead. Carson had loyally kept his mouth shut during the earlier troubles, but now he knew that the men had endured more than enough. If conditions were not going to improve very soon, the expedition would simply have to turn back whatever Frémont said.

Through the whirling, frozen snow they suddenly came to the crest of a rocky descent. A gust of wind momentarily drove the snowflakes aside. Far below them, blurred by mist, lay a splendid valley. Its great width seemed to stretch westward to a low and easy range of hills.

"I know it!" exclaimed Carson. "Fifteen years ago I went through that place. That's the Sacramento Valley ahead of us."

The news restored the men but not the mules. Most of the surviving animals were on their last legs. They were terrified and stubborn, preferring to remain where they were until they died. Yet somehow the men got them loaded and lined up ready to push onward. Emaciated, suffering from snow blindness and frostbite, staggering, they reached the slope and began to descend it.

They reached the first grass forty-eight hours

later. Their meal that night consisted of unsalted mule steak. By the end of the week they were comfortably encamped beside the Rio de los Americanos, which joined the Sacramento a few miles farther on. Deer were plentiful, and from a passing party of Indians they had even managed to obtain a couple of handfuls of salt.

Frémont had brought his expedition through the Sierras, but they had only just survived the journey. He had, in fact, run things much too closely. Several of his men had nearly lost their lives, but only one, the *voyageur* named Derosier, was thought to be dead. In a temporary fit of insanity he had strayed from the camp and failed to return. Nothing more was heard of him until two years later, when his memory suddenly returned and he found himself in St. Louis without the least recollection how he had arrived there.

The combined fortress-ranch of a great and famous character, John Sutter, stood close to the junction of the Rio de los Americanos with the Sacramento.

Sutter, a blond, short, heavy-bodied German-Swiss, had reached California by the Oregon Trail in 1838. After some extraordinary adventures he secured permission from the Mexican governor to acquire land and build a home. Sutter promptly set out to turn himself into a vast land-owner. With a land grant of 40,000 acres he be-gan to create a farm on which he raised wheat and cattle. The place had prospered from the start. Sutter had strengthened his position by giv-ing permission to a few hardy American settlers to establish themselves on small holdings on his land. In five years he had built a flour mill, a dis-tillery, a small canning plant, a blacksmith's shop, and a sawmill. By 1843, he was respected by the scattered American settlers and popular with the Mexican authorities. Sutter had become almost the king of everything he surveyed.

Frémont, who had heard of Sutter, led his men to the Swiss's hospitable estate. They were given a friendly welcome, tremendous meals of roast beef, vegetables, and fruit, and allowed to sleep in a warm, clean, comfortable bunkhouse. Mean-while Frémont was finding out everything he could from Sutter himself.

The 17,000 Spanish-Mexicans in California had no affection for the Government of Mexico. Although California was a province of that country, its easygoing inhabitants preferred to regard themselves as almost entirely independent. They had no wish to become involved in the tropical passions and murderous politics of Mexico proper. All they wanted was to be left alone in their elegant homes and gardens, to have their horses, their wines, the cool shade of their patios, and their numerous *fiestas*. As long as Mexican Government officials and American settlers alike did not make a nuisance of themselves, the native Californians were courteous and friendly toward everyone. Their attitude was an admirable one that deserved to endure. When they thought at all about more serious matters, many of these pleasant Spanish-speaking people believed that an American Government might tax them less harshly. The Americans, indeed, might even build a proper road or two or perhaps a real hospital. But conditions would be much more pleasant if both Mexico *and* the United States left them to go their own way and to run their own country.

The 400 Americans in California were naturally in favor of California's integration with the United States. They were not interested in what the inhabitants of the country thought or wanted. Governor Alvarado had been showing recent signs of animosity toward the Americans. Now he had forbidden new settlers to enter the country. A number of them who were ignorant of this order or had ignored it were arrested when they arrived. California, in fact, was in a state of turmoil. Nobody knew what was likely to happen next. The Americans, very unjustly, were feeling aggrieved because the Mexicans were trying to keep the country for themselves. Senator Benton and his friends shared the feelings of the ordinary settlers, but at least the Washington politicians were being cautious in the matter. It is most unlikely that even in secret instructions had they told Frémont to take a hand in forcing the issue.

Yet as soon as Frémont had rested his men at Sutter's ranch and re-equipped his expedition—including a new pair of boots for Preuss—he began to move southward along the western flank of the Sierras. His idea of crossing the Great Basin from north to south was abandoned. He was heading for an easy pass through the mountains that lay far to the south of the San Joaquin

River. On the way he passed a dusty little village of yellow-walled Mexican cottages, where hens scratched in the dust and pigs grunted in pens. The name of that coastal village was Yerba Buena. In later years it was to become the great city of San Francisco.

The Mexicans refrained from interfering with the expedition. They were growing accustomed to seeing strange Americans moving all over their country. The hotheads among them grumbled, but the older and cooler-tempered inhabitants were still trying to keep peace between the two countries.

To the east of Frémont now lay the Great Basin. He proceeded to lead his men into its wastes. With fresh supplies and good horses, they were confident of being able to look after themselves on their way across this desert.

The wilderness was much as they had expected: sand, yucca trees and cactus, lack of grass or other foliage for the animals, a great many dangerous snakes and whitening skeltons. Every now and then they caught sight of prowling groups of wild-looking, dark-skinned Indians. Not surprisingly the men rode with their rifles loaded and ready. Those Indians were obviously waiting a chance to attack.

If they had any doubts, the fact was made clear to them on April 25, 1844. Out of the glare and the heat and the loneliness of the cactus-dotted landscape staggered an elderly Mexican and a fourteen-year-old Mexican boy. They were crazy with thirst; their clothes were in rags.

After they had eaten and drunk and rested, Fuentes, the man, told the story of what had happened. His party had consisted of six persons: himself and his wife, the father and mother of the boy, Pablo, a man named Santiago Giacomo of New Mexico, and the boy himself.

Indians had suddenly appeared from nowhere. Fuentes and Pablo were out guarding the horses at the time. When they saw their camp attacked and overrun, they managed to escape on horseback. They rode for about sixty miles and then left their exhausted horses at a spring beside which grew a little grass. Since then they had been searching for help from any passing group of white men whom they might meet. They were certain that the rest of their party had been murdered.

Frémont's men listened to this story in silence. Then Godey, a trapper who almost matched Kit Carson in toughness, came with Carson himself to see Frémont. They were carrying their carbines, bandoliers of cartridges, and some food and water.

"The Indians around here have got to be taught to leave parties of white people alone," said Carson. "With your permission we'll go and give them a lesson."

The two men rode off into the desert. With them went Fuentes as guide. That night they camped among some dark and arid hills. Before dawn they were on the move again. Godey and Carson were now alone, as Fuentes' borrowed horse had gone lame. They sighted the Indian camp in the first light of the rising sun. Both men dismounted, tethered their horses, and checked their rifles. The Indians were eating an early-morning meal beside their campfire. They never observed their two enemies approaching under cover of bushes and rocks.

At a distance of forty yards Godey and Carson charged toward them, firing and running at the same time. Two Indians fell dead. The rest, screaming with terror, fled toward some nearby sand dunes while the heavy lead bullets of the carbines kicked up the dust beside them.

Godey and Carson wrecked the camp, smashed the cooking pots with a blow, and scalped the two dead Indians. They then rejoined Fuentes and carried on back to the camp.

"We gave those Indians their lesson," said Carson briefly.

The murder of the Mexicans took place in the desert in the northeasterly corner of Nevada. Frémont's men covered the distance to the tragic Mexican camp, which they reached on the evening of April 30. Frémont described the scene in his report on the expedition:

They were naked, mutilated, and pierced with arrows. Hernandez [one of the men] had evidently fought, and with desperation. . . . One of his hands and both his legs had been cut off. Giacomo, who was a large and strong-looking man, was lying in one of the willow shelters, pierced with arrows. Of the women no trace could be found, and it was evident that they had been carried off captive. A little lap dog which had belonged to Pablo's mother remained with the dead bodies, and was frantic with joy at seeing Pablo. . . . We rejoiced that Carson and Godey had been able to give so useful a lesson to these American Arabs, who lie in wait to murder and plunder the innocent traveler.

The expedition carried on the march toward the east. The heat seemed to increase with every day that passed. From midday until late afternoon the men lay in rough shelters and tried to protect themselves from the sun. Evening brought a cooler breeze and a swift drop in temperature. During the dark hours of the night the march went on under the brilliant starlight. As dawn began to brighten the eastern sky, camp was made and breakfast cooked. Fuentes and Pablo were still with Frémont's men. They had lost everything and were compelled to entrust themselves to the rough kindness of the Americans. Pablo had brought the dog with him.

In the swampy hollow of Las Vegas, where they found a spring of warm water but no fodder for their horses and mules, Indians attacked when they were least expected. Frémont had retired for an afternoon nap.

I fell asleep in the afternoon and did not awake until sundown. Presently Carson came to me and reported that Tabeau [a Canadian *voyageur*], who early in the day had left his post, and, without my knowledge, rode back to the camp we had left in search of a lame mule, had not returned.

They spent the next day looking for the missing man and discovered the tracks of the mule he was bringing back to the camp. Then, in a spot where the sand was scuffed and darkened with blood and dotted with sage bushes, they saw where Tabeau had stood and fought. They found four empty shells from his carbine, but the gun and the Iroquois tomahawk he carried in his belt were missing. So was Tabeau himself. "Horse, gun, clothes—all became the prey of the Arabs of the New World," wrote Frémont.

Preuss, who was normally an amiable sort of fellow, became as angry and vengeful as the rest of his companions. He never liked or admired the Indians he had met during his travels, and now he wrote in his diary with great bitterness:

> May God have mercy on the Paiutes who fall into our hands now. They lurk like wolves between the rocks along the road. Often we are surrounded by thirty or fifty of them without knowing it. One hears nothing, yet one is watched by a hundred

eyes. Woe to him who moves too far away from the party or accidently remains somewhat behind.

They were nearly across the Great Basin. Indians and cactus, sand and intolerable heat would soon be left behind.

On May 12, while they were crossing what is now the State of Utah, they came to a small river. Rich grass covered its banks. The famished horses and mules, scenting the water from afar, bolted toward it with their loads and flustered riders. That night the men bathed in cool water, washed their sweat-stiffened clothes, and prepared a special meal with some of their emergency rations.

A few days later they were rejoicing in the cool breeze that swept down nightly from the Wasatch Mountains. This was a more fertile and friendly region. The Paiutes had been left behind in their wilderness. Grass remained abundant, and game was becoming more frequent. Frémont's men began to climb the slopes toward the remote peaks, rejoicing that once again they shivered with cold beneath their blankets.

The rest of the homeward journey held no great difficulties or dangers. Across the Wasatch

Range and into Colorado they went, reveling in the sight of tall green trees and soft ground underfoot. Every evening they were able to shoot buffalo, and Fuentes proved himself a cook more expert than the rest of the men.

Toward the end of June, 1844, they reached Pueblo on the Arkansas River. Traveling faster now, eating good food daily, and with their animals refreshed and strengthened, another month's journey brought them to the Missouri River. A passing riverboat called at the stage to allow them to embark, and they voyaged downstream on deck. Fourteen months after they had set out with so much haste, they saw above the surrounding forest the distant houses of St. Louis.

The Benton family owned a large and impressive house in the city. From her bedroom window Jessie could hear the whistles of the distant steamboats while she spent her days awaiting her husband's return.

As those days turned to weeks and the weeks to months, she became more silent and thoughtful. Nearly a whole year had passed since she had last heard from Charles. She knew that during much of that time he had been crossing the Rockies, skirting dangerous Indian country and traveling in areas far beyond the frontier of civilization.

When the engines of Frémont's riverboat slowed and stopped beside the lamplit wharf, darkness had long since fallen on St. Louis. The time was nearly midnight. Most of the population lay asleep in their houses.

Frémont slung a small pack on his shoulders and set off on foot toward the Benton home. A few late passersby glanced incuriously at him in the occasional light from a wayside window or the infrequent oil lamps that scantily illuminated the streets. Once or twice they took a second glance. The bearded features, the deep-set eyes, and the small, quick-moving figure seemed familiar to some of these citizens. Before they could make identity certain, Frémont, moving lightly in his soft moccasins, had vanished into the darkness. A number of residents of St. Louis walked home in a thoughtful mood that night.

Jessie Frémont was not at the Benton mansion. She had gone to the home of a young girl cousin who was ill. Senator and Mrs. Benton were both asleep, and Frémont had no wish to arouse their household. He booked into an hotel and dropped onto the bed. It was the first time he had been able to relax completely in more than a year, and he slept deeply that night.

A strange rumor was circulating St. Louis next morning. Several citizens declared they had seen him. The servant at the Benton home to whom Frémont had spoken thought the same. But as the morning went on, he wondered whether he had seen a ghost.

"It looked like the Lieutenant," he declared. "But it was kind of dark in the doorway, and I didn't see his face properly."

Half of the city became certain Frémont was dead and that his ghost had walked the streets!

No one cared to break the news to Jessie. But in her cousin's house she heard the noisy sobbing of a good-hearted servant. As she was asking the girl the cause of her distress, the front door opened and in walked Frémont himself.

FIVE

Polk

THE SPANISH
OF CALIFORNIA

Back to Washington went the Bentons with Frémont. Then followed several peaceful months while he began to prepare his notes for the publication of a second report. The Senator had smoothed over the matter of the missing howitzer.

The appearance of this lengthy report was an important event in American history. It was read eagerly, not only by geographers but also by everyone interested in the far West and the Pacific

coast. Prospective settlers and their families strove
to obtain copies before they set out on their journey toward the distant Rockies. The Army Topographical Corps was highly gratified. Lieutenant
Frémont's excellent descriptions of unknown rivers and legendary lakes, of the extent of deserts,
and of the areas where water and grazing could
be found provided the entire American nation
with information for which it was hungry. The
Army's public image improved suddenly, although some of the senior officers were increasingly jealous of Frémont. They muttered irritably
that he had met with too much success for a
young man of thirty. They hinted that success
had come his way only because he was lucky
enough to marry a senator's daughter.

Their envy did no harm at all. The report continued to sell thousands of copies. Benton and his
friends began to plan eagerly for a third expedition. They knew that a great deal more territory
still remained to be explored and mapped thor-
oughly.

A period of great expansion was already under
way in the United States. The country was growing rapidly in size. The whole territory of Loui-

siana—which included the present areas of Arkansas, Missouri, Nebraska, Iowa, and South Dakota —had been bought from France in 1803. Florida had been ceded to the United States in 1819. Texas, which was formerly a Mexican state thinly populated by Americans, had declared its independence in 1836 after the tragic battle of the Alamo. It was now moving rapidly toward admission to the Union. The Territory of Oregon, which included the present states of Oregon, Washington, Idaho, and parts of Montana and Wyoming, was doing the same. President Polk was eager for the annexation of Texas and the control of Oregon. He was quite openly ambitious to seize California and, if possible, other Mexican territories as well.

Polk could have been more tactful and patient in carrying out his ambitious plans. But Polk, of Scots-Irish descent, came from Tennessee and was a slave owner. He had been brought up to despise those of darker skins. Thus, he was never able to look upon the Mexicans as a free and independent people with as much right as anyone else to their own country.

Frémont had never taken any great interest in

politics. He was now about to be drawn into the political web being spun by Polk, Benton, and other ambitious American leaders. (It should be said that Benton, a fair-minded, honorable man, objected to Polk's attitude toward Mexico.)

Frémont was first to receive recognition "for gallant and highly meritorious services in two expeditions commanded by himself." He was promoted to the rank of captain. Next he was escorted by Benton to the White House, where he had the honor of being presented to the newly inaugurated President.

Polk listened closely while Frémont spoke of the mountainous beauty of Oregon, of its fish and timber and wildlife. Next he described the sunny climate, the rich soil, and the splendid forests of California, and the suitability of the territory's coastline for the development of new harbors. Frémont showed the President certain official maps that had been printed ten years earlier. One of these maps even showed a river flowing from Great Salt Lake, through the Sierra Nevada, and into the sea at San Francisco Bay, and Frémont was able to point out the absurdity of such a claim from his own experience of those high mountains. The preparation of new official maps must be carried out.

Frémont was issued with orders for his third expedition. Polk and Benton still believed—quite wrongly as it happened—that England was planning to seize California and Oregon for herself. Frémont was therefore ordered to explore:

> . . . that section of the Rocky Mountains which gives rise to the Arkansas River, the Rio Grande del Norte of the Gulf of Mexico, and the Rio Colorado of the Gulf of California; to complete the examination of the Great Salt Lake and its interesting region; and to extend the survey west and southwest to the examination of the Cascade Mountains and the Sierra Nevada.

It seems likely that Frémont was given secret verbal instructions as well. The nation's relations with Mexico had become so unfriendly that shooting was expected to start at any time. Perhaps Frémont was told to pay particular attention to good trails by which American troops might move across country. Finally, it may have been hinted to him that in the event of an outbreak of war with Mexico, he and his men would be expected to give assistance to the American settlers in California.

So long as the politicians left Frémont alone with his surveying instruments, his *voyageurs*, and the empty horizon, he excelled as an explorer. But he was too high-mettled to act on behalf of shrewd, hard-bitten politicians with secret plans of their own. Those men would have been tenderfeet in a wayside camp. But in the stuffy salons of Washington they were on their own ground, and Frémont was the one who was out of his element. Perhaps by this time he had become a little too sure of himself, for apparently he never realized how completely he was being used by others.

Frémont seems to have acted on the secret instructions he was given. When he returned to St. Louis in May, 1845, he bought a number of the latest high-quality rifles. These weapons were issued to the sixty men he picked from the eager crowds of volunteers. Among those selected were many of his old companions including Godey, Basil Lajeunesse, and the hunter, Lucien Maxwell. Kit Carson, still in his beloved wilderness, was to join the expedition as it moved west. Preuss, however, was not there. He was married to a German wife with strong views of her own. She did not approve of a husband who went wandering all over the more dangerous parts of North America, sometimes even without shoes! Preuss was firmly ordered to remain at home and help with the children. His place was taken by Edward Kern, a clever young artist who was able to accustom himself quickly to the hard and dangerous life of the wilderness trail.

With his 60 men and 200 cattle, Frémont set out in July. By the end of August he had reached Bent's Fort on the Arkansas, where he replenished his supplies. The journey through the Rockies at the end of September was no hardship and left him with several days in which to make a fresh examination of Great Salt Lake. Thereafter, he crossed the sixty-mile desert to the west of the lake and so entered Nevada.

The days were growing shorter now that October had arrived. The party reached the Humboldt River, which flowed westward toward California. Frémont, anxious to save time, then divided his party into two groups. The larger party was to follow the river as far as Carson Sink, a westward journey of a couple of hundred miles. The artist Kern was to be in charge of this party. On reaching Carson Sink he was to swing southward along the eastern flank of the Sierra Nevada for a distance of about 100 miles. He was then to await Frémont at Walker Lake.

Frémont himself, accompanied by ten of his best men, set off on a southwesterly course that would take them across the detestable Great Basin. Frémont was out to find a better route across that wasteland. The skeletons he had seen by the wayside on his first and more southerly crossing of the Great Basin urged him on.

The route he took, from Franklin Lake to Walker Lake, turned out a success. In later years it was to become a popular and oft-followed trail by wagon trains. It was not a flat, desolate, and sun-scorched stretch of desert that he had crossed. To his surprised delight, he wrote to Jessie, it led through a series of low mountains:

> . . . their summits white with snow, while below the valleys had none. Instead of a barren country, the mountains were covered with grasses of the best quality, wooded with several varieties of trees, and

containing more deer and mountain sheep than we had seen in any previous part of our voyage.

When the two parties met at Walker Lake, Frémont had collected much fresh information about the little-known central parts of Nevada. The idea of dividing his expedition into two parts had worked so well that he decided to try it again.

Kern was to take the main party and head southward along the eastern side of the Sierra. On reaching a pass that was known to be usually free of snow, he was to swing westward through it. In the meadows and temperate sunshine of California, he was to make camp at a certain spot and await Frémont's arrival from the north.

Frémont had still not learned to treat the Sierras with respect. His courage was so high at times that it verged on the foolhardy. This time he headed for the Sierras and led his men into a pass that was later named Donner Pass because of a family that perished there.

Frémont and his fifteen men were again lucky. They traversed the pass without any trouble. The weather remained bright and cold, but there was almost no snow. They came out on the western slopes and began to descend toward the great pine forests and shining stretches of rich green grass. December 10, 1845, saw them once again eating and drinking within the friendly walls of Sutter's Fort.

This journey by Frémont across the northern end of the Great Basin resulted in one of his most famous discoveries: a new and reasonably safe route between Great Salt Lake and northern California. Unfortunately, the route did not become known to westward-moving settlers as quickly and as widely as it deserved.

While at Sutter's Fort, Frémont heard the latest news. Exciting events had been taking place in California since he was last there in the spring of 1844.

The native Californians had decided to stage their own revolt against the Mexican governor in the autumn of that year. The Government in Mexico City was beginning to take a last-moment interest in California, a fertile and prosperous region they had carelessly neglected for the past 100 years. Large parties of Mexican soldiers were sent there. As these troops were seldom paid, were badly equipped and ill fed, it was only natural that they began to help themselves on reaching California. Cattle and foodstuffs, farm produce and private property began to disappear. Taxes were increased, and the enraged Californians were harshly ordered to pay them or go to jail. Their protests against the thievery were ignored by the Mexican authorities. Tempers rose, and the Californians decided to take matters into their own hands. Leaving their shady patios, their haciendas, their guitars and beloved horses, they staged a rebellion against Governor Micheltorena with an energy and spirit that surprised that dictatorial military gentleman. He was obliged to return southward, taking his available soldiers with him. California suddenly became an almost independent province of Mexico.

It was a dangerous state of affairs for the Spanish-speaking native Californians. As long as their province had been nominally part of Mexico, the United States was reluctant to interfere with them. Now, by their own action, they had become an almost independent little country with a few thousand inhabitants. They were nearly helpless in the face of the American hunger for expansion, but they refused to acknowledge the fact. They hoped that having beaten General Micheltorena and his ragamuffin troops, the United States would be so impressed that California might be left alone. They had chosen to break away completely in a gallant but forlorn effort to stand on their own feet.

"As a people, they believe in the democratic theory that all men's heads are the same height," Sutter told Frémont. "But the trouble with them is that every man among them believes his own head is just a little higher than that of everyone else! Now that they're all happy at having driven out Micheltorena, they're liable to start quarreling among themselves over jobs in their own civil administration."

Frémont went on south to meet the rest of his party, but on reaching the agreed meeting place, he found the men under Kern had not arrived. His own party was in the San Joaquin Valley, where the Indians were hostile and cunning. They made repeated attempts to steal Frémont's horses and to cut off any of his men who lagged behind. On several occasions they had to be driven off with rifle fire.

While awaiting the arrival of Kern, Frémont took time off to visit the little Spanish town of Monterey. Below low green hills he saw picturesque adobe houses with roofs of brown tiles. The two principal streets ended beside a couple of wooden wharves lapped by the clear blue waters of the Pacific Ocean. There were shady, flower-filled gardens, groves of wide-spreading trees, and a little yellow stone fort on a low cliff. The native Californians were an indolent people, but they had a Spanish love of elegance and beauty. Monterey in those days was the most delightful place that Frémont had seen.

The rest of the expedition finally arrived. They had mistaken the meeting place and were finally guided to it by Carson and his friend Owens, who had been searching the countryside for them. Frémont was again in command of sixty well-armed men. They were encamped near the area still held by Mexican troops.

Neither the Californians nor the Mexicans welcomed the sight of this "small army" of Americans riding at ease through the country they regarded as their own. It was a matter on which both sides could agree. Within a few days a young Mexican officer rode into Frémont's camp and handed him an official package covered with red seals. Inside was an elegantly written document containing the Mexican governor's order to depart from California at once.

If Frémont had been in command of troops, he might have been justified in refusing to obey the order. But he was officially engaged as an explorer and had received no written orders to undertake military duties. The men under him were not soldiers but civilians. He seems to have relied on the secret verbal orders—whatever they were—that had probably been given to him, and he believed that Washington would give him full support for any actions he took.

In any event, Frémont did not obey but instead marched his party to the top of a hill called Hawk's Peak, fortified his camp, and raised an American flag from the top of a forty-foot pole. Not surprisingly Californians and Mexicans rose in wrath at Frémont's action.

Frémont remained on his hilltop for three days. In the valley below, a number of hastily assembled Mexican soldiers and a growing number of Californians prepared to launch an attack. Heavy guns began to appear in the valley. When those weapons opened fire, Frémont's improvised fort would be in trouble.

Perhaps the cool night and sharp breezes, as much as the sight of the ranging guns, cooled Frémont's hasty patriotism. He began to wonder if he had not acted too hastily. On the third night, he abandoned his position and began to retreat northward.

No one had been hurt during the stupid affair, but Frémont's men lost considerable popularity with the Californians. They were roughly dressed, bearded fellows slung with rifles and pistols. Whenever they appeared in a district, private property began to vanish, along with a certain number of cattle and pigs. The Californians wondered if the Americans as a people were any better than their own crooked officials and thieving soldiers.

Frémont led his men back to Sutter's Fort, where he remained for a while. Soon he noticed that the friendly Sutter had cooled toward him and his men.

Frémont had become confused. His intense love for honest, selfless exploration was now

mixed with a personal ambition to acquire land and perhaps wealth for himself in lovely California. Constantly in his mind were the secret instructions given him in Washington. He may have known already that the United States intended to seize California. Perhaps he did not wish to miss a chance to acquire property for himself.

Frémont was a poor man. He had nothing except his modest Army pay and the limited extra allowances he was receiving for his work as an explorer. No one could blame him if he saw in California a chance to become a landed proprietor and able to provide a good home for himself and his family.

But for the time being, California seemed to be quieting down. Frémont finally came to a decision. On April 24, he began to carry on with his normal work. They marched northward past Yerba Buena and along the Sacramento River. Frémont's intention was to obey his orders to explore the Cascade Range.

Unknown to him and his men, on the day they began their northward journey, rifle fire was echoing along the banks of the Rio Grande. General Zachary Taylor's soldiers were in contact with the soldiers of Mexico. Nineteen days later, on May 13, 1846, the United States declared war. Reluctant to fight a war but determined to defend their country, the Mexican Government made a similar declaration on May 23.

SIX

Stockton

MIDNIGHT ATTACK

They ran into bad weather near Lake Klamath, 400 miles north of Yerba Buena. Snow alternated with lashing, icy rain. Indian and game trails were blocked with fallen trees, displaced boulders, and muddy craters worn by flooding, roaring streams.

Under such conditions no camp could have been comfortable. The men crouched in leaky, uncomfortable tents and tried vainly to dry their clothes over damp and smoky campfires. Game was scarce. They were tired, cold, and dispirited. They had lost their enthusiasm for exploration. Like Frémont himself, they had an idea that things were going to happen in California before long. They wanted to be on the spot to take a hand in whatever developed. In the meantime, they missed the warm sunshine and drier climate of the coast.

They were eating a lumpy and unpleasant supper around their campfire on the evening of May 8 when they heard a distant shout. Two riders appeared from the darkness. One was a farmer named Samuel Neal, on whose ranch Frémont had spent a night while making his way north to the Cascade Range. His companion was another local farmer.

"A young Lieutenant Gillespie, of the Marine Corps, is at my house," Neal told Frémont. "I've fixed for him to stay there while I came on up here to find you. The Indians make this countryside too dangerous for anyone who doesn't know it properly. We had to shoot a couple who tried to attack us yesterday."

"Where's Gillespie from?" asked Frémont.

"Washington," said Neal. "He says he's got

official dispatches for you. He's been traveling for I don't know how long. He speaks Spanish and passed through Mexico to the West Coast. Then he found that the quickest way to get to California was to sail to Hawaii and then come back on another ship. Gillespie reached Monterey a few days ago and has been traveling north ever since. Until he met me, the last news he had of you was at Sutter's Fort."

They set off at daybreak the following morning. Before sunset they had covered nearly fifty miles. Unknown to them, Gillespie was cautiously advancing northward, accompanied by six reliable Indian guides. He had grown impatient while waiting for Frémont to arrive and with more bravery than common sense had decided to ride out to meet him.

The two parties met on a dark and winding trail through the pine forests close to the southern end of Lake Klamath in Oregon. Gillespie handed over a bundle of letters. Some were from Jessie and her family. Among the rest was a sealed package from Secretary of State James Buchanan.

The contents of that official letter remain a secret. But Gillespie confirmed the rumor that

Neal had already mentioned to Frémont. The United States was about to declare war on Mexico; in fact, the proclamation had probably already been made. (It was actually issued on May 13.) Buchanan was inviting the Californians to make an official declaration of their independence of Mexico. Once they had done so, their state would be invited to join the Union.

Whatever Buchanan had written, it prompted Frémont to take swift action. His whole party was to return southward into California. What he intended to do with his little force of well-armed followers when he reached his destination remains unknown. Perhaps Frémont had no definite plans. The two parties made camp for the night. They were all tired after an exhausting day's travel. Frémont was busy reading and rereading his letters. Possibly he did not pay his usual strict attention to the mounting of guards. Even Carson, the man who never relaxed while he was on the trail, seems to have omitted some of his usual vigilance. Years afterward he said:

> That was the only night in all our travels, except the one night on an island in the Salt Lake, that we failed to keep guard. The men were tired, and we

expected no attack now that we had fourteen [it was actually seventeen] in the party.

The Klamath Indians were lurking in the depths of the restless, sighing forest. They were a war party out for mischief, particularly dangerous because they were armed with the barbed iron arrowheads and light steel axes obtained from British trading posts in the north of Oregon.

The Indians crouched among the trees while the men ate their evening meal, smoked their pipes, and began to spread their blankets. The fire around which they slept was banked with pine logs. Silence gradually descended on the camp. The Indians began their silent advance. No one heard them approaching. Carson described what happened next:

Owens and I were sleeping together, and we were waked at the same time by the licks of the axe that killed our men. At first I did not know it was that; but I called to Basil [Lajeunesse] who was on that side: "What's the matter there? What's the fuss about?" He never answered, for he was dead then, poor fellow—and he never knew what killed him. . . . The Delawares (we had four with us) were sleeping at that fire and they sprang up as the Klamaths charged them. One of them, named Crane, caught up a gun, which was unloaded. He couldn't do much with it, but he kept them at bay fighting like a soldier, and did not give up until he was shot full of arrows, three entering his heart.

Carson was on his feet in a moment. Owens jumped up beside him.

"Indians!" they shouted. They aimed and fired at the dusky figures running in the red glow of the fire. Grabbing at the pistols lying under their saddle pillows, they fired again. Frémont came charging out of his little shelter with a heavy six-barreled (pepperbox) pistol in his hand. The rest of the men prepared to join in the fight with gun, knife, pistol, and clubbed carbine. Carson's account continues:

> I think it was a fellow called Stepp who killed the Klamath chief, for it was at the crack of Stepp's gun that he fell. He had an English half-axe slung to his wrist by a cord, and there were forty arrows left in his quiver, the most beautiful and warlike arrows I ever saw. . . . When the Klamaths saw him fall, they ran; but we lay, every man with his rifle cocked, until daylight, expecting another attack.

When cold, gray daylight spread over the forest, the men saw that three of their companions, including Basil Lajeunesse, had been killed. The other two were the Delaware named Crane and an unnamed Indian of that same tribe. The half-awakened white men had shot wildly and inaccurately in the dying glow of the fire, but at least they had killed the Klamath chief.

Carson went on the warpath. Throughout his life in the wilds he never allowed himself to be attacked without striking back at those who attempted to destroy him. He chose ten of the most fearless men, including Godey, Maxwell, and Owens, all of whom were handy with their rifles. They rode out of the camp and headed for the shore of Lake Klamath. As they rode a circuit of this stretch of water, they sighted a village of the Klamath Indians. Carson ordered a halt while every man checked his rifle, his pistol, and his knife. Then, galloping at full speed, shooting and yelling, they swept down on the village.

Their shooting this time was better. Several of the Indians were killed, but Carson did not pause to count them. He and his companions dismounted, set fire to the place, and waited until the houses were a mass of flames. Late that afternoon they returned to the camp.

As Frémont rode out to meet them, a lone Klamath warrior suddenly rose to his feet from behind some cottonwood bushes where he had been crouching. Carson jerked up his rifle but the cartridge misfired. The Indian drew back the string of his bow and was about to release the shaft when Frémont, who had spurred his horse, Sacramento, into a sudden gallop, rode him down.

"I owed my life," said Carson later, "to them two. The Captain and Sacramento saved me."

The expedition rode on southward beside the Sacramento River and entered California. Now they were able to obtain the latest news.

The Mexicans had decided—when it was too late—that California was a province worth saving for their country. Army detachments had been hurriedly sent north to man crumbling little adobe forts. A new governor, Don José Castro, had taken up his headquarters at Monterey. The American settlers were in a truculent and impatient mood. The native Californians were divided and uncertain what to do. The more ambitious, or perhaps the more practical, ones among them felt that if they had to choose between Mexico and the United States, then the Americans would be preferable. Roads, hospitals, reasonable taxes, an improved system of justice—and perhaps even better jails—were thoughts that still appealed to them. On the other hand, the Americans they had seen so far seemed little better than wild, lawless brigands.

The local Indians, many of whom had received a smattering of education at the missions, were mostly degenerate and brutal. Under the influence of the white man's liquor they were capable of committing the worst crimes. During the present confusion in California, and the lack of any efficient system of law and order, they began to loot farmhouses, burn crops, steal crops, steal cattle, and murder any settler who tried to defend his property. These Indians were loosely combined in a war party of about 600 warriors.

The 800 Americans in California were delighted to see Frémont return to the province. Eagerly they waited to see what he would do. His rank of captain in the United States Army carried great weight with them.

Frémont learned that the little fort of Sonoma, twenty miles north of the village of Yerba Buena, was being used by Governor Castro as a military storehouse. The fort had whitewashed adobe walls reinforced with balks of roughhewn timber. It was square, with a flat roof of tiles. The floors were made of brick. The garrison of Mexican soldiers was slovenly and careless, the inevitable result of neglect, bad food, and arrears of pay. No one could expect such troops to fight gallantly to defend the country that treated them so indifferently. In any event, they were almost totally illiterate and had no clear idea where they were or what their duties were supposed to be. They were mostly peasants who had been kidnapped in the fields and villages and forced to join the Mexican Army. Their one great ambition was to get back to their farms as quickly as possible.

Frémont detailed a man named Ezekiel Merritt to take fifty men and capture the Sonoma fort. This band of adventurers walked into the place at dawn on June 14, 1846. The sleeping Mexicans were too surprised to resist.

The haul of weapons included some brass cannon, a great many antique muskets, a couple of hundred pounds of lead for casting bullets, and a barrel of black powder. The soldiers were set free. When last seen, they were on their way southward, back to Mexico and their farms.

The officers were a different case. They had a sense of duty, they belonged to the regular Army, were paid more or less steadily, and were certainly a great deal better fed. General Vallejo, the commander of Sonoma, accompanied by his officers, was taken under escort to Sutter's Fort to remain as a prisoner of war.

It was bad luck for Sutter. He had always been on friendly terms with the Mexican authorities. Through their kindness and help he had obtained his enormous landholdings. Whatever the Americans intended to do with California, he preferred to remain neutral. Sutter knew that Vallejo had always shown friendship toward Americans and now owned a ranch of which he was extremely proud. There was no reason for such a distinguished man to be interned as a prisoner of war. Angry words were exchanged between Frémont and Sutter, and their friendship ended on that day.

The Americans who took over the Sonoma fort decided to design a flag for themselves. They obtained a piece of white cloth, drew a star in its upper right-hand corner, and in the center depicted a grizzly bear. Across the bottom of the flag were printed the words: *California Republic*. On June 14, 1846, this flag was first flown from the fort. The fighting that was to follow became known as the Bear Flag War.

The continuing confusion in this new republic was leading to considerable lawlessness. Both sides indulged their touchy feelings with noisy and unnecessary gunplay. Meanwhile, Frémont went off to Yerba Buena in a small boat and sabotaged the Mexican guns he found there in a small, unguarded fort. He then moved down the coast and entered Monterey on July 18, accompanied by 160 riflemen. Governor Don José Castro had conveniently left the little town.

Frederick Walpole, a British Naval officer stationed in Monterey, described the arrival of Frémont and his men:

> A vast cloud of dust appeared first and thence in long file emerged this wildest wild party. Frémont rode ahead, a spare, active-looking man. . . . He was dressed in a shirt and leggings, and wore a felt hat. After him came five Delaware Indians who were his

bodyguard. . . . The rest of the men, many of them blacker than the Indians, rode two by two, the rifle held by one hand across the pommel of the saddle. . . . The dress of these men was principally a long loose coat of deerskin, tied with thongs in front; and trousers of the same, of their own manufacture. They are allowed no liquor. No doubt this has much to do with their good conduct.

This was the California Battalion, a fighting force that passed into history and legend and was considerably polished up in the process. Undoubtedly they were motivated by patriotism, but every man among them probably had his eye on some neat parcel of land he hoped to obtain for himself when the present troubles ended. They were ready to fight, and fight hard, to make sure of their acres. They had the spirit of their pioneering ancestors who first crossed the Appalachian Mountains to settle in the broad and fertile valleys of the Mississippi. Nothing was going to prevent them from building their farms and homesteads.

They got what they wanted. Governor Castro quickly realized the impossibility of holding California in the face of this armed rising. He was short of troops, munitions, and money. The order was issued for a general retreat of all the troops under his command.

The Bear Flag War seemed almost at an end. General Zachary Taylor, who was to become the twelfth President of the United States in two years' time, was advancing southward deep into the heart of Mexico. Another American invasion force, under General Winfield Scott, had landed in Veracruz and was about to march on Mexico City. Far away in Washington, Secretary Buchanan and the British ambassador had signed a treaty by which Oregon was partitioned at the forty-ninth parallel. The Americans thereby gained the territories of three future states, namely Idaho, Washington, and Oregon. (Idaho was admitted to the Union in 1890, Washington and Oregon in 1889 and 1859 respectively.)

Meanwhile, life for Frémont was growing more complicated. He was an honorable patriot, but his speedy successes in California had caused him to grow overconfident. The news had just reached him that he had been promoted to the rank of lieutenant colonel. It was a swift promotion for a man who was still only thirty-four years old and did nothing to increase his popularity with the regular Army officers.

At the same time General Stephen W. Kearny was advancing westward with an army of about 2000 American troops. He captured Santa Fe from the Mexicans and moved on across New Mexico to conquer—as he thought—California.

The aging Kearny was not the right man for the job. He was obstinate, fierce-tempered, jealous of his rank, a brave soldier, but not a particularly good military leader. During his westward march, he met Kit Carson riding eastward with dispatches from Frémont. The scout told him that the fighting in California appeared to be dying down; the country was fairly safely in American hands.

Kearny decided to send back his troops and retain merely a hundred cavalry as his escort into California. Though reluctant, Carson was obliged to turn back and act as a guide for the general's detachment.

Kearny reached the California frontier to the east of San Diego at the beginning of December, 1846. There he was joined by another sixty

American volunteer riflemen, who brought the news that fresh fighting had broken out in the province. The native Californians had endured enough troubles. Their resentment toward be-whiskered American adventurers who were claiming ownership of their country had risen swiftly. Combining with such scattered Mexican soldiers as they could find, they rose at last in fiery, patriotic mood to defend their native California.

Carson tried to warn Kearny. "If you care to remain here, sir," he said, "I can slip across the country to the American force at San Diego. They'll be able to send you men as reinforcements."

Kearny chose to ignore this advice. With 160 men and 2 howitzers he crossed into California.

His advance guard was promptly wiped out in a furious charge by the splendid horsemen of the Mexican cavalry. Shaken and staggered, the Americans pushed on across the country. Every patch of cover and every hilltop seemed to conceal a sniper. On a small hilltop farm named San Bernardo, the general realized to his disgust that he could go no farther. The Mexicans had completely surrounded his little force. His men were short of water and almost out of rations. Unless help came quickly, he and his men were sure to be either captured or killed.

Carson had been right after all!

Red-faced, dusty, and ill-tempered, the general sent for the scout. Carson was given instructions to try to make his way at night through the enemy's lines and obtain help from San Diego.

Carson, using his skill and woodscraft, succeeded in slipping away. He reached San Diego and gave the alarm.

One hundred and eighty men of the California Battalion rode out of the town. Slouched in their saddles, rifles resting on the pommels, as bearded, untidy, and fearsome as ever, they sent their horses loping across California toward the beleagured General Kearny. They reached the San Bernardo ranch within two days.

The Mexicans decided not to risk a battle with these veteran frontiersmen. They slipped away in the night and faded into the silence of the hills.

The general pulled himself and his escort together. He had lost twenty-five of his men, and he had been rescued by an undisciplined force of

ruffians. In a furious temper, he marched on to San Diego, where Commodore Robert F. Stockton was awaiting him.

Stockton was the commodore of two American Naval vessels, *Congress* and *Cyane*, which had arrived on the West Coast. He was an honest, ambitious, up-and-coming officer. Acting on orders given him by his superior officer, Stockton had joined forces with Frémont at the beginning of the Bear Flag War.

As the senior officer on the West Coast, Stockton had promised Frémont the governorship of California when the country was restored to peace. Until then, however, Stockton was acting as governor and commander in chief, Frémont as military commandant of California. The system worked well. Frémont and Stockton were on the best of terms with each other. Then Kearny arrived in a general's uniform and a violent temper. Within a couple of days, he and Stockton began a violent and unending quarrel. The general wanted to be the kingpin. He insisted on holding the ranks of governor and military commander. Stockton, who had formed no high opinion of Kearny, was bitter and reluctant.

Frémont, writing later, said:

When I entered Los Angeles, I was ignorant of the relations existing between these gentlemen. I had not received from either of them any order or information which might serve as a guide in the circumstances. Upon my arrival I waited upon the governor and commander in chief, Commodore Stockton; and a few minutes later called upon General Kearny. I soon found them occupying a hostile attitude, and each denying the right of the other to assume the direction of affairs in this country.

The squabble went on almost daily, even after January, 1847, when the rebelling native Californians agreed to peace terms. "We now have the prospect of having peace and quietness in this country," Kearny wrote in a dispatch, "which I hope may not be interrupted again."

There was not much hope of peace in his own office. Stockton was an obstinate and competent New Englander. Irish-American Kearny was hot-tempered. Frémont was equally hot-blooded and used to having his own way. The mixture was about as explosive as possible.

Kearny stuck to his conviction that it was up to him to organize a civil government—a job he would probably have done with success. He refused to recognize Commodore Stockton's present rank. Frémont was caught between the two of them while still remembering that he himself had been promised the governorship.

The unfortunate row was caused by a careless lack of cooperation between the Army and Navy Departments in Washington—in addition to the differing temperaments of the men concerned. The Navy had ordered Stockton to administer California. The Army had ordered Kearny to do the same. Frémont had his own private orders from the politicians.

The final explosion came when Frémont told Kearny that he intended to side with Commodore Stockton. It was unwise of him; he was an Army officer, and General Kearny was his superior officer.

Matters became worse in February, 1847. Kearny received fresh orders from Washington. They were brought around Cape Horn by the frigate *Independence*. It was President Polk's wish, said the dispatch, the Kearny should become governor and commander in chief of California.

The general was delighted. He did not, however, inform Frémont and Stockton of the contents of the President's letter. He kept the matter a secret to himself. Frémont continued to show loyalty to Commodore Stockton but not to General Kearny. He did not know that the general was now officially the governor of California.

Frémont's political friends were neglecting him. Events were taking place so fast in California that his own past services were ignored. But when the War Department received the latest and most up-to-date news from the West Coast, Frémont was suddenly remembered. Senator Benton was probably the man responsible. The Secretary of War dispatched fresh instructions to Kearny in which the latter was directed:

> To employ him [Frémont] in such a manner as will render his services available to the public interest, since he has an extensive knowledge of the inhabitants of California.

Kearny ignored this directive. He was busy informing the commanders of Naval vessels arriving on the coast of his promotion to governor of California. Among those he told was Thomas

Larkin, the American consul at Monterey. It was probably from Larkin that Frémont finally learned the truth: Washington had chosen Kearny instead of himself. On hearing this news, Frémont reluctantly agreed to give up his position as governor and to recognize the general's supreme authority.

If Kearny had been a prudent man, he would have allowed the quarrel to end there. But he was jealous and vindictive and believed that he could bring charges of disobedience against Frémont. The explorer, he declared, had refused to obey him after he, Kearny, had been made governor and commander in chief. Kearny ignored the fact that Frémont had been entirely in ignorance of his promotion to that position.

Throughout April and May, 1847, Kearny continued to behave badly toward Frémont. The explorer did his best to endure being ignored and even insulted by Kearny, but his hot temper led to stormy words between them. These scenes increased the general's desire to bring Frémont before a court-martial.

Kearny decided in June to return eastward and make his report to Washington. He ordered Frémont to accompany him, and he forced him to leave behind a large amount of his scientific equipment.

Only nineteen men left in Frémont's party. The rest decided to remain in California. The troops under Kearny naturally supported their commanding officer. Frémont's men continued loyal to him. On the long return march, each party built its own campfires, ate its own provisions, and slept in two groups. When they reached Fort Leavenworth in Kansas, Kearny sent for Frémont and ordered him to consider himself under arrest. The general added that Frémont should consider himself free in the meantime to take his own men back to St. Louis and pay them off.

Jessie was awaiting him in that city. She and her husband had not met for two years. Rumors regarding the young explorer's troubles in California with Kearny soon spread through the city. Men came to shake his hand; strangers visited him at the Benton home to express their sympathy. His own men offered to appear as witnesses. Jessie wrote hastily to her father. The Senator wired back to say that he would stand by his son-in-law and was already in touch with the War Department. But whatever other political friends Frémont may have had, they did not appear now. They were all lying very low indeed.

It was a sad ending to Frémont's third and most successful expedition.

SEVEN

Kearny

DEATH IN THE ROCKIES

Kit Carson came east to Washington to give evidence on his leader's behalf. The broad-shouldered, taciturn frontier scout was hospitably entertained at the Benton home. He was granted an interview with President Polk, his evidence was taken down in writing, and he was carefully questioned by Senator Benton. When all this was done, Carson set out on his return journey to the West Coast. He was more convinced than ever

141

that the pleasures of civilization were not for him. Life was much safer beside a campfire in the forests or prairies!

The charge against Frémont was mutiny. He had refused to recognize General Kearny as governor of California. Frémont's defense was that Commodore Stockton had been commander in chief during the Bear Flag War. In January, 1847, the commodore had issued a proclamation declaring that Frémont was to become governor and commander in chief of California. At that time Kearny and his soldiers had just been rescued from the San Bernardo ranch. The general had left both him and Stockton in ignorance of the orders he received later from Washington by which Kearny himself was made governor and commander in chief.

Kearny lost his temper in court. Arrogant, bitter, and ill-natured, he created a poor impression in the minds of the spectators. Public sympathy with Frémont continued to rise, and Kearny lost much of his reputation. But the strict and often unjust Army discipline of those days prevailed in the end. A senior officer must always be supported against a junior officer. Whatever the reasons, Frémont had disobeyed Kearny's orders.

On January 31, 1848, the court found Frémont guilty on three counts. He was sentenced to be dismissed from the service. Six of the thirteen Army officers who served on the court-martial recommended clemency. They were not convinced that Frémont was actually guilty of mutiny, disobedience, and unbecoming military conduct.

President Polk was not happy about the whole affair. He countermanded the punishment of dismissal from the service. "Lieutenant Colonel Frémont," he directed, "will resume his sword, and report for duty."

The prospect of the trial had been too much for Frémont's aging mother, the lady of good Virginia family. She died in Charleston soon after learning that her son had been placed under arrest.

Frémont himself believed that he had been ill-treated. He would not accept the decision of the court against him and resigned his commission in the Army.

Frémont's action did his reputation among the

American people no harm at all. They regarded him as the hero of California. In February, 1848, a defeated Mexico gave up all claim to Texas, California, Arizona, New Mexico, Utah, and Colorado. In return, the United States paid Mexico $15,000,000. Most Americans believed it was wrong that such splendid results should be overshadowed by the probably unjust sentence passed on Frémont. Their feelings rose higher when, in August, 1848, Kearny was promoted to the rank of major general. He died later that year in St. Louis.

Frémont was left a poor man. Like thousands of others in his plight, he decided to seek his fortune in California. Before leaving the West Coast he had deposited $3,000 with Thomas Larkin, the friendly American consul at Monterey. Larkin was to keep his eyes and ears open and try to buy some land on Frémont's behalf.

Frémont also had another project. Financiers and civil engineers were already discussing the idea of building a railroad across the North American continent. They were worried by the thought that in winter the track through the

Rockies might be blocked with snow. Frémont's idea was to find a route that would remain open during even the coldest months. If he succeeded in taking an expedition through some such pass in the depths of winter, surely the railway builders would be encouraged to adopt that route.

The entire country became interested in the idea. Thousands of Americans began to dream of the day when they might roll westward along steel rails to establish new homes and farms for themselves and their families on that far-off sunny coast beside the warm and friendly waters of the Pacific.

A number of financiers agreed to put up the money for a new Frémont expedition. Their confidence in him was undiminished; they admired the way in which he had stood up to the harsh treatment handed out to him by the Army. The necessary funds were forthcoming, but they were not overgenerous. Rich men are careful when deciding how much money they should hand out for any worthy purpose.

Frémont assembled thirty-three men at St. Louis. Once again many of them, such as Godey, were his companions of former expeditions.

Preuss, his genial face beaming, turned up. Kit
Carson was not there. He had moved on to California with the intention of settling down with
his family on a new ranch.

The expedition, with the usual horses, mules,
and creaking carts, reached Bent's Fort on November 16, 1848. Frémont was not happy as he
observed the weather. There were signs that the
approaching winter would be very harsh indeed.
Sheets of ice were floating on the river. The night
wind blew with a cutting, ferocious cold. Snow
already lay almost two feet deep on the ground,
and the solid mass of the Fort was already half
hidden in steep drifts. But up to the present things
had gone well with the expedition. Encouraged,
Frémont was not in a mood to hesitate tackling
the Rockies, the great mountains he had always
managed to challenge successfully in the past.
His diary entry for November 17, 1848, reads:

For a distance of 400 miles our route led through
a country affording abundant timber, game, and excellent grass. We find that the valley of the Kansas
affords by far the most suitable approach to the
mountains. The whole valley soil is of very fine

quality, well-timbered, abundant grasses, and the route very direct. . . .

Both Indians and whites here report the snow to be deeper in the mountains than has for a long time been known so early in the season and they predict a severe winter. This morning for the first time the mountains showed themselves, covered with snow, as well as the country around us, for it snowed steadily the greater part of yesterday and the night before. . . . I think that I shall never cross the continent again, except at Panama. I do not feel the pleasure that I used to have in these labors . . . and as I find I have these no longer, I will drop into a quiet life.

On November 21, the expedition reached the cluster of small, roughly built huts with smoking stone chimneys that was Pueblo, in Colorado. About a hundred people lived there. Most of them were Indians, but there were also a few wrinkled and bent old white fur traders, who carried in their memories a half century of hard practical experience.

"Don't try to make the crossing this late in the year," they warned Frémont. "Best dig in here and wait until the warmer spring weather returns to these parts."

It is easy to say that Frémont should have taken this advice. But if he had always listened to the warnings of others, he would never have become an explorer. He was out to prove that a pass through the Rockies would remain open for a railway in winter. He did, however, get one of the Pueblo veterans to act as his guide.

This man was known as Old Bill Williams. Sixty-two years old, he was tall, lean, wrinkled and as tough as seasoned hickory. Long ago he had come westward from either Missouri or Tennessee and still spoke with a Southern drawl. He chewed plug tobacco, wore a leather deerskin shirt, much stained and frayed, and a strange fur cap he had made for himself. He was an excellent shot with his ancient musket, and he had fought Indian war parties more times than he remembered. According to the men who knew him best, there wasn't much of the honest veteran about Old Bill. He was a dangerous old rogue, not above eating human flesh when rations grew a bit short.

"In starving times," Kit Carson once said grimly, "no one who knows him cares to walk in front of Old Bill Williams."

In time to come, Frémont regretted selecting Old Bill as a guide. He wrote in a letter:

> The error of our journey was made when we engaged this man. He proved never to have in the least known, or entirely to have forgotten, the whole region of country through which we were to pass. We occupied more than half a month in making a journey of a few days, blundering our way through deep passes, for which we were obliged to waste time in searching.

With Williams slouched in the saddle of a spare horse, the men left Pueblo on November 30. Before they had traveled more than a couple of miles, they were enwrapped in a storm of sleet.

Deep in the Sangre de Cristo Range of central Colorado, Williams began to show signs of hesitation as to the route to follow. The men's confidence in him decreased more quickly than Frémont's.

"Bill definitely missed the promised *good* pass," wrote Preuss on December 15, 1848. "Again we had to struggle a lot with snow and tree trunks."

Meanwhile, the mercury in the thermometer had sunk so low that it no longer registered the

temperature. The men began to suffer from frostbite. Several of the mules lay down and refused
to move another step. The men shot them, hacked
off as much meat as they could carry, and plodded
on upward to the cloud-wrapped backbone of
the snow-covered mountains.

They reached the summit of the first range on
December 16.

"Hands and feet, ears and noses of some of
our men were frozen," said Preuss. "That old
fool Bill lay down and wanted to die just at the
summit. Many animals perished here."

They stumbled down the slopes into a river
valley. They were nearing the headwaters of the
Rio Grande. The temperature was a little higher,
and the mercury began to register at the bottom
of the scale. Frémont wrote:

> High, precipitous, and frozen mountains were
> behind us and a broad dreary plain before us, and
> the Rio Grande fifty miles ahead. . . . We traveled
> late and camped in the middle of it, without any
> shelter from the winds, and with no fuel but some
> wild sage, a small shrub which grew sparsely
> around. The cold was intense, the thermometer

tonight standing at 17 degrees below zero, and it was so cold during the day that Ducatel, a young fellow, came very near freezing to death.

They kept going until they reached the Rio Grande. Ahead of them, like a giant prison wall, rose the San Juan Mountains, which comprise the highest mass of the Rockies. Choked with snow, enwrapped in mist and flurries of sleet, they rose 12,000 feet above the valley toward a freezing leaden sky.

Old Bill was laconic but obstinate. He declared that if they made for his Wagon Wheel Pass, they could still get across the mountains. He had discovered the pass himself; he could find his way through it at any time.

A modern historian has suggested that Williams was unaware that Wagon Wheel Pass was impassible in winter snow, that he seems to have started toward it, then turned unknowing into rough mountain territory. Probably this is about what happened. The aging frontiersman would never have led the way deliberately into unknown country in the depths of a bitter winter. He knew these mountains too well.

But the true reasons for that mistake were never known. Men who knew the Rockies said that Frémont must have ignored Williams' advice when the going became worse. They declared that Old Bill "would never have run into the death trap," that Frémont "picked out the route which he wanted to travel over the mountains" and refused to abandon it when conditions became impossible.

The men were now in the Arctic depths of the La Garita Mountains, forty-five miles in width. No pass to the west existed anywhere.

By Christmas day the men, muffled in blankets, leather jackets and woolen jackets, were half dead from cold, exhaustion, and hunger. They were eating mule flesh and sleeping in deep holes created in the snow by their blazing fires. Most of the animals were dead, the rest were so worn out that they might be expected to die at any time. Only then did Frémont decide to turn back.

Four of his best and most experienced men volunteered to set out by themselves for the nearest settlements in New Mexico. They would buy fresh mules, load them with rations, and bring them back up the Rio Grande Valley to an agreed meeting place. The leader of this four-man party was Bill Williams.

Next morning Frémont organized the rest of the men's retreat. Conditions were so bad, the men so exhausted, that they could travel at the rate of only one mile per day. Faster progress might have been made if Frémont had decided to sacrifice the baggage, but he was determined to take it with him.

Wrote Preuss:

> We had to leave the animals behind. It was impossible to drive them through the snow. To take meat with us seemed to be too troublesome because we already had plenty to drag. Moreover, we could now expect relief in about a week.

They lost one man during that retreat. Raphael Proue collapsed and died of cold. Stumbling, suffering from frostbite and snow blindness, the rest of them arrived back in the Rio Grande Valley.

Another disaster was awaiting them. All the deer had moved south because of the bitter weather. They were reduced to their last rations, some macaroni, sugar, a little coffee, and a few slices of salted pork. Hurriedly they made a rough camp, kindled fires, and awaited the arrival of the rescue party. They were slowly starving to death.

A lone, wandering Ute Indian saved them on the sixth day. He led them to a tiny camp of his own people a few miles away.

Godey was able to shoot a deer, and on January 17, 1849, Preuss wrote:

> Miserable as the place looked, we prepared here a wonderful breakfast of corn mush and venison, together with our coffee.
>
> When we walked to the next grove, what did we find? Three of the men we had dispatched for relief. They were crouching round a fire, devouring dried deer meat. We had to open our eyes wide to recognize them, so skinny and hollow-eyed did they look. . . . King [one of the four] had died of exhaustion and the others had eaten part of his body.

The Indian looked at the scanty remainder of the party's food stocks. "We will guide you to the nearest settlement," he declared. "The sooner we leave, the better. If we remain here doing nothing, we will all die."

Frémont set out with the Indians, accompanied

by Godey, Preuss, and a hardy fellow named Saunders. Two days later the men left behind decided to follow after their leader down the valley. They might save some time as they would meet the returning rescue party. All they now had left to eat were a few handfuls of sugar, four pounds of macaroni, and a few scraps of frozen mule flesh.

They began their march on January 20. Two or three of the men collapsed and had to be left behind. Next morning the survivors shot two grouse and ate them raw. Later that day they found a dead wolf, which they also devoured.

Frémont was traveling fast on the few thin and miserable horses belonging to the Indians. He reached Taos in six days. The local population, both American and Mexican, began to arrange a speedy rescue. Writes Preuss:

They had flour and goats, but there was a lack of mules. The next morning Godey rode fifteen miles further in order to rent some at another settlement. He returned with thirty animals and several Mexican drivers. During this time our hosts were also making bread from coarse flour. Godey had also bought a hog, the larger part of which was cut up.

On the last day of January, the half-dead survivors were still managing to stagger on southward among the pine trees of the Rio Grande. A far-off rifle shot echoed crisply across the snow. Then came a second shot, followed by a faint shout. A long mule train came into sight. Riding alongside the animals were Godey and the Mexican drivers. As they caught sight of the distant scarecrows reeling, and sometimes crawling, toward them, the rescuers began to reach into their saddlebags for bread, packets of smoked ham, and slabs of pork. Far in the distance, more snow-coated figures were still appearing. It took Godey nearly two days to collect the survivors. Wrote Preuss in his diary:

> They were rather scattered. . . . Nine more had already said good-bye to this life. This means that eleven out of thirty-three, exactly one third of the entire personnel, had died of starvation. . . . The deep snow made it impossible to get at the baggage. Hence I am here, as poor as Job. Nothing saved except what I have on my body and the few blankets. But to have saved one's life is the best; the rest may be retrieved again.

EIGHT

Frémont

GOLDEN SUCCESS

The men slowly recovered in Taos. As they grew stronger, so did the arguments and accusations. Some of the men were bitter and critical of Frémont. They declared that his crazy idea of crossing the Rockies in midwinter had caused the loss of life. Others said that Bill Williams was the man responsible for the disaster. The men's confidence in Frémont as a leader was shaken. Some of them declined to accompany him any further. Among these were Edward M. Kern the artist, his two younger brothers, and Bill Williams. Others who were anxious to reach California, or still retained faith in Frémont, were prepared to continue.

(When spring came in that year of 1849, Williams and Kern found their way back to the abandoned camp in the mountains. Kern was anxious to recover his pictures and painting materials. Old Bill probably had his own ideas about loot. Hostile Indians were awaiting them. Both men put up a fight, but they were finally overwhelmed and killed.)

When his party reached California by a southerly route through Arizona, Frémont received what at the time he believed was a fresh disappointment.

Larkin, the consul with whom he had left $3,000 for the purchase of land, had bought a vast tract in the Sierra Nevada, 100 miles inland from the coast. It was not what Frémont had wanted. He had planned to settle with Jessie in some grassy valley above San Francisco, where fruit trees, vegetables, and livestock would flourish. The land bought by Larkin was named Mariposa, which means *butterfly*. It was said not to

be fertile. Hostile Indians roamed freely throughout the remote region. Frémont was sure that he
could not take his town-bred wife, accustomed to
ease and elegance, into such a wild and dangerous
region.

Other news was more cheerful. Almost a year
previously, on January 24, 1848, a man named
James W. Marshall was erecting a sawmill in
partnership with Sutter on the American River,
a branch of the Sacramento.

Marshall found gold. The whole of California
promptly went mad with gold fever. News of
the strike spread eastward by sailing ship or was
passed back from one advancing caravan of wagons to another across the prairies. From the deep
South, from the eastern seaboard, from lonely
hamlets along the banks of the St. Lawrence
River, a great and swelling horde of men began
to pour westward. Most of them—the wiser ones,
who generally arrived—followed the routes that
Frémont had explored and mapped.

California became front-page news. During
that year of 1848, 100,000 new settlers arrived
there. Jessie, too, came west with their daughter,

taking the commercial route across the Isthmus of Panama, and joined her husband in San Francisco. As quickly as possible the Frémonts left the noise and squalor and disorders of the city. Back they went to the little town of Monterey. A hospitable Californian family had offered them a comfortable, flower-filled home.

While Jessie remained with these new friends, Frémont rode inland across the arid San Joaquin Valley and into the foothills that lay to the east. The Mariposa Grant, as it came to be known, delighted and surprised him. There was rich shade on those slopes. Streams of fresh, sparkling water, with shady pools under the trees, gushed down the hillsides. Pine trees abounded and springy, fresh grass. Dark soil and sun-filled meadows met his gaze everywhere. Here was a perfect site for a ranch, a ranch that could spread in future years over all the 40,000 acres.

He made another trip to the coast and brought back Jessie and their daughter. He had underrated his wife. She was delighted with the unspoiled beauty of Mariposa and eager to settle there as quickly as possible. Even though she was the city-bred daughter of a senator, Jessie had inherited the blood and spirit of her pioneering ancestors.

Competent Spanish carpenters—men who had wisely refrained from the dangers and hysteria of the gold rush—came inland to erect a solid wooden house. Jessie and eight-year-old Elizabeth camped in a pleasant spot among the trees, close to a stream. It was a busy, pleasant, and relaxed time for Frémont. At last he could spend his leisure with his family.

Then an unexpected development occurred. Gold was found in Mariposa—not just traces of gold such as men were scrabbling for along the American River, but gold in such enormous quantities that the Mexicans stared with incredulous eyes. Almost overnight Frémont became a very wealthy man, a man who was on his way to being a millionaire.

He was not accustomed to wealth; the simple, inexpensive life he had always led was comfortable enough for him. As a rancher he would certainly have prospered and enjoyed a good life with his wife and family. But the sight and feel of that gold began to cast dark shadows over his life in the years ahead.

In accordance with Mexican law, which was still being observed, Frémont might be the owner of the land, but he did not hold the exclusive rights to minerals. A mob came pouring across the San Joaquin Valley, hot with greed and haste, blind to the beauty of the scenery and the purity of the crystal streams. The whole Mariposa Grant, all 40,000 acres of it, was quickly overwhelmed by these human ants. They hacked and dug, cut and blasted. They speedily reduced its loveliness to a litter-strewn shambles.

Frémont's men, armed with rifles and shotguns, managed to hold back the hordes from his own diggings. But the gold seekers tore up his new fences and killed the cattle he had bought. There was no law and order in California during that era. No police had yet arrived on the scene.

Frémont's takings from his diggings proved fabulous. The gold his workers brought out was stored in 100-pound deerskin sacks, each of which was worth $25,000. "But the beautiful vision he had formerly entertained," declared a writer who lived during that same period of history, "was destroyed by the discovery of gold. It threw farming projects out of the question altogether."

California became the thirty-first state in 1850. Frémont was elected a Democratic senator. Political duties made it necessary for him and his wife to return to the east. Mariposa was left in the care of a manager, backed up by many of Frémont's friends from the days of the California Battalion.

Meanwhile, questions about his legal ownership of Mariposa were being raised. Congress in 1851 refused to confirm any Californian land claims without legally written deeds. All the Mexican archives were in a state of chaos. Many documents were lost. For the first time Frémont found himself wondering whether he would be able to hold on to his ranch. The placer gold deposits were nearly exhausted. There was gold-bearing quartz rock on the land, but it would require heavy and expensive machinery to extract it.

Frémont decided against buying that machinery with his own money. His great wealth had given him false confidence in his ability as a businessman. Actually he had no experience in business at all. He instructed an agent named Hoffman to go to England and arrange for mining companies in that country to obtain leases on the Mariposa Grant. He then created a muddle by giving almost identical instructions to another man named Sargent. Working without each other's knowledge, Sargent and Hoffman finally discovered that they were selling leases on the same land. A furious quarrel began. Frémont had to cancel his plans.

Frémont then had another run of bad luck. In 1851, he was defeated for reelection by proslavery forces. In June of that same year a valuable house Frémont had bought in San Francisco was destroyed in the Great Fire.

The cool-headed Jessie realized that her husband was becoming involved in too many matters, none of which he properly understood. It was time he rested for a while. "Let's go to Europe," she suggested. "We've been through enough during the past few years. I'm sure we've earned a holiday for ourselves."

They crossed the Atlantic in the 1,500-ton sidewheel steamer *Africa*, belonging to the famous Cunard Line. It was a strange choice of vessels. In 1851, two comfortable steam-heated steamers, the *Atlantic* and the *Pacific*, belonging to the American-owned Collins Line, were attracting the fashionable American traveling public. The Cunard ships were safer, but they were cold, primitive, and lacked any bathrooms.

American friends welcomed the Frémonts in London. They traveled on to Paris, leased a house in a fashionable quarter of the city, hired excellent servants, and made a number of friends.

Late in 1852 they decided to return to the United States. While stopping off in London, Frémont and his wife were invited to dine one evening with some friends. Four uniformed constables, accompanied by a lawyer's clerk, appeared as he was handing Jessie into a carriage outside their exclusive hotel. He was taken to jail. The charge against him was that of nonpayment of $15,000 that, during the Bear Flag War, he had drawn in drafts on James Buchanan, the Secretary of State at that time, to cover the expenses of the California Battalion. The warrant had been issued by the merchant who had cashed

Frémont's drafts. Congress, with inexcusable care-lessness, had neglected to authorize payment.

While Frémont was spending the night in prison, Jessie hastened to the home of the American ambassador in London. Bail was immediately forthcoming, and Frémont was released the following morning. Congress finally got around to settling the debt the next year.

When the American public heard of this scandalous business, the national temper rose. One American writer commented:

> This was one of the rewards Frémont received for having won California for his country. To be publicly thrown into a British prison, and submitted to ignominy and outrage in the streets of London. What rendered the occurrence particularly annoying was the fact that Colonel and Mrs. Frémont had just before been honored by the Queen [Victoria], with a reception at a Drawing Room, of which the usual announcement had been made in the public Gazettes.

No happiness awaited their return to the United States. Jessie's brother, Randolph Benton, had died during her absence in Europe. Jefferson

Davis, Secretary of War, had ordered five separate surveys to be made in order to find the best route for a transcontinental railway. Army officers of much less experience than Frémont had been placed in command of the survey parties. Frémont himself was entirely ignored. Jessie had given birth to a daughter named Anne Beverley in Paris. Soon after their return to Washington, the child died.

A point had come in Frémont's life when a steadier and more thoughtful man might have thought seriously of retirement. He was still a millionaire and could afford to be independent of everybody and everything. But Senator Benton, as tireless and outspoken as ever, was busy with fresh plans for his son-in-law. He was about to take what he believed to be an important step to strengthen Northern interests against those of the South.

Benton knew that Davis, a Southerner, favored a railway along the thirty-second parallel (Mississippi-Louisiana-Texas). Benton and his fellow-Northerners wanted a route that ran somewhere near the thirty-eighth parallel (Missouri-Kansas-Colorado-Utah). In order to find such a route, these men chose Frémont to lead an expedition, which a number of industrialists were again prepared to finance.

Frémont was forty years old. He himself knew that he was past his prime as an explorer. All the territory he would cover had already been explored by others. But perhaps he was tired of politics, disappointments, and litigation. He may have felt a sudden yearning for the simple life of the saddle and the campfire.

Charles Preuss certainly felt the same way. He was as restricted by his marriage as ever. His German wife still disapproved of the idea of her husband wandering all over the wilderness. She again refused to let him accompany Frémont. When Preuss finally realized that his free and adventurous days were ended forever, he committed suicide.

The fifth and last expedition consisted of twenty-two men, including Delaware Indians and two Mexicans. None of Frémont's old companions seem to have rejoined him. The party set off westward in August 1853, only two months after their leader had returned from Europe.

They reached Bent's Fort at the end of November. From there the route led up the Arkansas River to the Sangre de Cristo Mountains. The weather remained reasonably mild and the temperature above freezing while they went through the Cochetopa Pass at the northern end of the range.

It looked as though it would be a perfectly safe journey. Only a light covering of snow lay on the ground during the early days of December. Conditions were less favorable on the semidesert western side of the mountains. The expedition was now venturing into little-known and dangerous country. The cold became intense, food ran short, bands of Ute Indians hovered in the distance and watched from morning to night. Starvation gradually descended on the party and daily the cold became worse. Finally they reached the hospitable Mormon village of Parowan in Little Salt Lake Valley. Frémont wrote:

> We were forced to abandon all our heavy baggage to save the men. I shall not stop to send back for it. The Delawares all came in sound, but the whites of my party were all exhausted and broken up, and more or less frostbitten. I lost one, Fuller, of

St. Louis, Missouri, who died on entering this valley. He died like a man, on horseback, in his saddle,
and will be buried like a soldier on the spot where
he fell.

They left Parowan in February, 1854, and
continued westward across Nevada's Great Basin,
of bitter memory. As a result of the generous
rations given by the kindly Mormons, the men
continued to eat well, and the desert Indians left
them alone. They finally reached the Californian
frontier between Yosemite and Death Valley.
The Sierra Nevada was deep in winter. The men
eyed the white-capped summits, shrouded at frequent intervals by heavy flurries of sleet and
wind-whipped snow. They drew closer to the
heat of their campfire and turned their backs on
the grim sight. A winter crossing was not for
them. They knew that their leader had almost
died of cold and starvation in the Rockies only
six years before.

They need not have worried. Frémont had at
last learned to respect those pitiless mountains.
He was no more anxious than the men to cross
them at this time of the year. They swung south

until they came to Walker's Pass, which they traversed without the least trouble. By the middle of April, 1854, they were in San Francisco.

(The route he followed on this fifth and last expedition was never used by the railway builders, although the Santa Fe line passed through much of the territory he had recommended. The Union Pacific used a more northerly route through the high Sierras—a route of which Frémont always disapproved.)

The American press and public regarded Frémont more highly than ever. They knew that he was rich and happily married. They thought much of the fact that he had gone back voluntarily to the hardships of exploration. Once again he had given his services to the country without hope of reward. Such popularity brought no happiness to Frémont's private life, however. The dark shadows around him continued to increase.

Mrs. Benton, who had always been his good friend, died in 1854. Senator Benton, a sturdy opponent of slavery, lost his seat in the Congress in the feverish election that same year. The political atmosphere in Washington became unfriendly toward the Frémonts. Jessie pleaded with her husband to leave the capital. Before they departed, the Benton home caught fire and was totally destroyed. Far away in California, troubles were increasing on the Mariposa ranch. Dangerous crowds of squatters were continually trying to take over the whole estate. Frémont found it necessary to go back to the West Coast and chose to go by the Panama route.

In the fall of 1855, the Democratic Party offered him the nomination for the Presidency. He refused. Soon afterward the newly formed Republican Party made the same offer.

Frémont already had too much on his mind and too many interests. Now, more than ever before, the time had come for him to drop out of public life, invest his wealth, and settle down to a quiet family life. But he was never a man who could relax in pleasant idleness.

He accepted the Republican nomination, much to the delight of the press and the antislavery faction. The Civil War was looming on the political horizon, and the whole country was excited and divided in opinion.

There were thirty-one states in those days. Buchanan (the Democratic candidate) carried nineteen. Frémont carried eleven, and Fillmore, a candidate for a hastily formed political party called the Know-Nothings, carried one. Buchanan gained 174 electoral votes, Frémont 114, and Fillmore 8.

With the loss of the election, Frémont's political career was ended. He was probably glad. He had never understood the hard, ruthless world of politics. He had formed few friendships with the politicians. He preferred the straight-speaking people of the farms and frontier.

In that same year of 1855, the Supreme Court upheld his claim to the Mariposa estate. Frémont had finally bought the ore-crushing machinery with his own money, and gold was still being produced at the rate of about $3,000 per week. The constant ugly threats and occasional violence of envious and jealous prospectors continued to prove a nuisance, but Frémont believed that as law and order spread throughout California, the disturbances would die down. He continued to live with his wife and daughter in the ranch house he had built in earlier days. Two sons remained at school in the east.

The period from 1858 to 1859 was perhaps

the happiest in Frémont's life. He was respected throughout California and becoming richer all the time. Jessie, who had always been delicate, was growing stronger in the pleasant climate and had come to love California.

However, costs were rising at the mine. The yield of gold was again decreasing. Taxes in California had increased to an almost crippling amount. The time came when Frémont realized that in spite of the clatter and thump of his machinery, in spite of his contented and friendly workers, he was no longer making an appreciable profit from the mine. The ravaged and broken hillsides, the felled trees, and the polluted streams seemed to be taking their revenge.

Then came the news of the bombardment of Fort Sumter on April 12, 1861. The United States plunged into the ruinous heartbreak of the Civil War.

Frémont was in Europe again when the war began. He was attempting to raise a loan by public investment for the purchase of gold-mining machinery even more efficient than the plant he had already installed. As soon as the news of the war reached him, he dropped everything and hurried home. By June, 1861, he was reinstated in the Union Army and promoted to the rank of major general.

Dapper, bearded little General Frémont arrived at St. Louis in July. He was the newly appointed Commander of the Department of the West.

The once friendly city was silent and tense in the damp heat of midsummer. The Unionists had stopped Missouri from seceding, but the Confederate element was powerful, vindictive, and dangerous. Recruitment for their troops was being carried on openly in the streets. The colors of the Confederate flag were visible on many flagpoles. Missouri, which had a population of over a million, was deeply Southern in its outlook, traditions, and history.

"I have given you *carte blanche*," Frémont quoted President Lincoln as saying to him. "You must use your own judgment and do the best you can."

There was little that Frémont could do when he arrived. He lacked almost everything necessary to hold Missouri against the dashing and fast-moving Confederates. Jessie described his situation in a letter to a friend:

> An arsenal without arms or ammunition—troops on paper and a thoroughly prepared and united enemy. Thick and unremitting as mosquitoes. The telegraph in the enemy's hands and the worse for us as not being avowed enemies. . . . I have begged Mr. Frémont to let me go and tell [the President] how things are here. But he says I'm tired with the sea voyage—that I shan't expose my health any more and that he can't do without me.
>
> It's making bricks without straw out here and mere human power can't draw order out of chaos by force of will only.

Jessie was right. Frémont lacked uniforms and money, food, horses, wagons, and rifles for his men. His recruits often went barefooted, drilled with sticks or ancient swords, were seldom paid, and even strove to get hold of sixty-year-old English Brown Bess muskets. Down in south-western Missouri, Confederate bands were swarming across the countryside, burning farms, dynamiting bridges, and derailing trains.

To make matters worse, Frémont lacked experience as a military commander. By personality and improvisation he managed to hold the northern half of Missouri against the Confederates. He procured rifles by one means or another, some bought with his own money. He fought endless paper battles with the War Department in Washington and worked sixteen and seventeen hours a day.

He made mistakes, of course. Any other raw officer would have done the same, and all of them did. But his actions and motives were often deliberately twisted by his political enemies. Among those enemies was the powerful Blair family, consisting of a father and two sons, who had strong economic and political interests in Missouri. Corruption, bribery, and muddle made Frémont's duties even more difficult. At no time, however, was he involved with the large-scale swindlers and profiteers who were defrauding the Union Government in exchange for worthless goods and worn-out horses.

Frémont's greatest mistake, in the eyes of President Lincoln and his war Cabinet, was the proclamation he issued to place all of Missouri under martial law. Any unauthorized person found with a rifle in his hands behind the official lines of the

Union Army would be tried by court-martial and, if guilty, shot. The proclamation added that slaves and property belonging to any inhabitant of Missouri known to be hostile to the Union should be confiscated. The slaves would then be declared free.

Lincoln wrote a tactful letter to Frémont, in which he said:

> I think there is great danger that the closing paragraph [of the proclamation] in relation to the confiscation of property and liberating slaves . . . will alarm our Southern Union friends and turn them against us; perhaps ruin our rather fair prospect for Kentucky.

Lincoln asked Frémont to modify the proclamation. But Frémont believed that his proclamation was right. He could not agree with the President's mild suggestion. Most of the ordinary men in the street and the soldiers of the Union Army also supported his view.

Surly, incompetent, or jealous generals, rotten wagons supplied by dishonest contractors, political enemies, and untruthful letters that were turning the President against him became too great a burden for Frémont to bear. Yet before he left the Army late in 1863, many of the country's political leaders had begun to take his side. They resented the way in which Frémont had been starved of men, supplies, and money and then blamed for not doing more than he had done. He was actually offered another and more suitable command in the field. At the same time it was made known to him that there would soon be a seat in the Cabinet if he wanted it.

Frémont refused both offers. He had learned enough about politics and politicians. He was weary of their interference in military matters.

"With a feeling of joy akin to ecstasy," wrote Jessie, "I heard his decision to remain in private life."

If Frémont had collected all his available wealth and invested it securely, the remaining years of his life with Jessie would have been tranquil and pleasant. He was no longer a millionaire but at least he was still a very rich man—not rich enough perhaps to continue to finance the growing expenditure on gold production from Mariposa, but with sufficient wealth to purchase a gracious home in California.

Unluckily for him, the prospect of comfortable retirement did not appeal to his active mind. Again he plunged into the dangerous world of high finance.

Frémont was no match for the robber barons he came up against. In a series of complicated transactions, through the issue of dubious shares, and a great many misleading promises, they finally caused him to lose control of the Mariposa Grant. The tycoons and their lawyers then gathered in court for the final kill.

Frémont took the stand himself, but he was reluctant to accuse the men who had trespassed on his trust. He emerged from that court a very much poorer man. He was no longer the owner of Mariposa. The shares now all belonged to men who were smarter, more experienced, and completely ruthless.

Someone then suggested that he should interest himself in railway speculation. Again the venture ended badly. The modern railway bandits took him for the last of his wealth. A graying veteran of sixty, Frémont was a completely ruined man.

Jessie was the one who earned the money for

several years thereafter. Shrewder than her husband in her knowledge of men and politics, she also excelled her husband in her skill as a writer. Books and articles, essays and stories began to flow from her pen. Eventually she was able to double the miserable salary of $2,000 a year that Frémont was earning as the territorial governor of Arizona, a position he had been offered in 1878, when he was sixty-five years old.

When he resigned from that position in 1883 because the dry climate did not suit his wife's health, they moved to a little cottage on Staten Island. Jessie continued with her writing. Their two sons, Frank and John Charles, Jr., went into military service, one to the Naval Academy, the other to the Military Academy. Frémont himself settled down to writing his autobiography.

Memoirs of My Life: A Retrospect of Fifty Years was published in 1887, when Frémont was seventy-four years old.

The book appeared too late. A younger generation was not interested in explorers and exploration. People were going everywhere by train or steamer, and the whole of North America was mapped. The public had not yet realized the great and colorful history that was made in Frémont's lifetime. As a result, the book was a failure. The planned second volume was never published.

Frémont and Jessie returned to the warmer climate and fresh sea breezes of the little town of Los Angeles. Somehow they raised the money to buy a pleasant little cottage in a flower-filled garden, where they settled down to spend their last years together.

Consciences began to stir in Washington. Older men who studied history and were perhaps more leisured and humane than their predecessors gradually remembered the great old explorer. In 1890, Congress invited him to New York and voted to have the name of John Charles Frémont restored to the Army lists with the rank of major general. The pension for which he became eligible amounted to $6,000 a year. It was a handsome income in those days. For the first time in twenty years, Frémont and Jessie could cease to worry about money.

But Frémont never returned to Los Angeles. While he had been in England years before, an English lady had asked him to visit the grave of her little son, who lay buried in Brooklyn. With his usual kindliness, Frémont agreed to her request.

He went to the grave, bearing a wreath of flowers, on the little boy's birthday in July. The day was hot, and he caught a chill while returning to his boarding house. A doctor was hurriedly sent for. He arranged for telegrams to be sent to Frémont's sons, but only John Charles, Jr. arrived in time. Three thousand miles away from his beloved wife in California, Frémont the explorer died that same night.

In the little cottage on Oak Street in Los Angeles, Mrs. Frémont lived on alone. There were no more financial worries for her; she received a pension of $2,000 a year payable to the widows of Army generals. Her married daughter, Elizabeth, visited her frequently, and the old lady was greatly respected and loved by the whole town. She was dignified, witty, and perceptive. Many of her callers were leading men in politics and finance. They found themselves charmed and fascinated by Jessie Frémont's memories, which covered nearly seventy years of a vanished age of American history. Los Angeles mourned greatly when the splendid old lady died in 1902. She and John Charles Frémont lie buried side by side on a hillside at Piermont, New York, overlooking the Hudson River. The grave is marked with an impressive granite and bronze monument. It consists of a flag and a sword, and also an engraved portrait of Frémont himself. On the granite is carved a long inscription that tells the story of his achievements.

To refer to Frémont as an explorer is not altogether correct. During his expeditions he certainly covered vast regions of almost unknown territory, but in nearly every instance some wandering trapper or prospector, perhaps a man like Kit Carson, had traveled that way before.

His greatest achievement was the discovery of new and safer routes across those dangerous stretches of country. He surveyed and mapped so that those who followed in his footsteps could travel in safety. His life was more that of a pathfinder than explorer. The countless dusty wagons that bore men, women, and children westward across the continent to California were guided by Frémont's practical and careful observations.

They always knew where grazing areas lay, where sweet water and firewood could be obtained, and the most suitable fords in the rivers they must traverse. Those early settlers owed a great deal—perhaps sometimes their lives—to Frémont.

After Frémont and the rolling, creaking wagons, accompanied by men with rifles, came the railways. They were built across much of the country he surveyed, including Pueblo, the Sangre de Cristo Mountains, the Gunnison River, and Salt Lake City. But as civilization rolled westward along those humming, shining rails, the buffalo and the Indians, the men like Carson and Godey and the Canadian *voyageurs*, vanished into the yellowing pages of history. Little more than twenty years after the first transcontinental train smoked and clanked and whistled its way westward, Frémont himself was dead.

Jessie Frémont was the one who, in a single short sentence, composed the most accurate and matchless tribute to her husband's achievements:

From the ashes of his campfires have sprung cities.

BIBLIOGRAPHY

Frémont, John Charles, *Memoirs of My Life: A Retrospect of Fifty Years*. Chicago and New York: Belford, Clarke & Co., 1887.

Nevins, Allan, *Frémont, Pathmarker of the West*, Vols. I & II. New York: Frederick Ungar Publishing Co., Inc., 1939.

Upham, Charles Wentworth, *Frémont's Life, Explorations, and Public Service*. Boston: Ticknor & Fields, 1856.

GENERAL BACKGROUND

Ghent, W. J., *The Early Far West. A Narrative Outline, 1540-1850*. New York: Longmans, Green & Co., 1931.

Thwaites, R. G., ed. *The Original Journals of Lewis and Clark*, 7 Vols. New York: Dodd, Mead & Company, 1904-5.

Turner, F. J., *The Frontier in American History*. New York: Henry Holt & Co., 1920.

Ronald Syme's early days were spent in an old castle in his native Ireland. Before he was nine he had the free run of the library in his home, thereby acquiring a love of reading. In later boyhood, he spent a few years in New Zealand, mostly hunting wild pig and trout fishing with his sports-loving father. At eighteen he went to sea and visited many parts of the world. About the same time he began writing short stories and feature articles. In 1934 he left the sea to become a journalist. During World War II Mr. Syme first served as ship's gunner, but later transferred to the British Army Intelligence Corps in which he saw service in North Africa and Europe.

Today Ronald Syme, a well-known author in both England and the United States, lives in the peaceful South Pacific island of Rarotonga. His home is a century-old, white-walled stone house within two hundred yards of a beautiful lagoon. The shelves of his library are lined with books, and he can check almost any historical fact he needs for his writing. He enjoys, he says, "most of the advantages of civilization without the corresponding disadvantages."